WEEKEND

BOOK OF

SCI[illegible] FICTION

COMPILED BY STUART GENDALL
ILLUSTRATED BY REGINALD GRAY

PUBLISHED BY HARMSWORTH PUBLICATIONS LTD.,
FOR ASSOCIATED NEWSPAPERS GROUP LTD., LONDON

WEEKEND BOOK OF SCIENCE FICTION

ISBN 0 85144 180 7

MADE AND PRINTED IN GREAT BRITAIN BY
THE GARDEN CITY PRESS LIMITED
LETCHWORTH, HERTFORDSHIRE SG6 1JS

CONTENTS

Page

Look, you think you've got troubles, *Carol Carr* 6

Security, *Brian M. Stableford* 17

I, Mars, *Ray Bradbury* 20

Great lost discoveries I – Invisibility,
Fredric Brown 29

The sixth palace, *Robert Silverberg* 31

The day Volman died, *Philip Dunn* 41

Computers don't argue, *Gordon R. Dickson* 46

Great lost discoveries II – Invulnerability,
Fredric Brown 59

An honest day's work, *Harry Harrison* 60

Action replay, *Richard Quarrie* 69

The yellow pill, *Rog Phillips* 74

Great lost discoveries III – Immortality,
Fredric Brown 85

The Nothing, *Frank Herbert* 87

Mix-up, *George Collyn* 96

Time fuse, *Randall Garrett* 106

It's a *good* life, *Jerome Bixby* 111

The End, *Fredric Brown* 126

ACKNOWLEDGEMENTS

Grateful acknowledgement is made for permission to print the following stories;

"It's a Good Life" by Jerome Bixby.
Copyright 1953 by Ballantine Books.
Reprinted by permission of the author and the E. J. Carnell Literary Agency for Forrest J. Ackerman.

"I, Mars" by Ray Bradbury.
Copyright © 1949 by Ray Bradbury.
Copyright renewed © 1977 by Ray Bradbury.
Reprinted by permission of the author and his agents Abner Stein Ltd.

"Great lost discoveries; Invisibility, Invulnerability and Immortality" and **"The End"** by Fredric Brown.
Copyright 1961 by Fredric Brown.
Reprinted by permission of the author's agents A. M. Heath & Co. Ltd.

"Look, you think you've got troubles" by Carol Carr.
Copyright 1969 by Damon Knight.
Reprinted by permission of the author and her agents, Andre Deutsch Ltd., from *Orbit 5* edited by Damon Knight, 1970 edition.

"Mix-up" by George Collyn.
Copyright 1965 by George Collyn.
Reprinted by permission of the author and his agents MBA Literary Agents, Ltd. First published in *New Worlds* 1965.

"Computers don't argue" by Gordon R. Dickson.
Copyright 1965 by The Condé Nast Publications, Inc.
Reprinted by permission of the author and the E. J. Carnell Literary Agency.

"The day Volman died" by Philip Dunn appears for the first time.
Copyright 1981 by Philip Dunn.

"Time fuse" by Randall Garrett.
Copyright 1954 by Randall Garrett.
Reprinted by permission of the author and his agents A. M. Heath & Co. Ltd.

"An honest day's work" by Harry Harrison.
Copyright 1973 by Harry Harrison.
Reprinted by permission of the author and his agents A. P. Watt Ltd.

"The Nothing" by Frank Herbert.
Copyright 1973 by Frank Herbert.
Reprinted by permission of the author and his agents John Farquharson Ltd., from *The Book of Frank Herbert* published by Granada.

"The yellow pill" by Rog Phillips.
Copyright 1953 by Ballantine Books.
Reprinted by permission of the author and his agents A. M. Heath & Co. Ltd.

"Action replay" by Richard Quarrie appears for the first time.
Copyright 1981 by Richard Quarrie.

"The sixth palace" by Robert Silverberg.
Copyright 1965 by Galaxy Publishing Corporation.
First published in *Galaxy*.
Reprinted by permission of the author and his agents A. M. Heath & Co. Ltd.

"Security" by Brian M. Stableford.
Copyright 1979 by Cosmic Perspectives Ltd.
Reprinted by permission of the author and his agents MBA Literary Agents Ltd.

SCIENCE FICTION has been a popular form of entertainment ever since Mary Shelley wrote "Frankenstein" in 1818. Its theme of a scientist's own creation turning against him mirrors our modern dilemma: when will all the super-sophisticated machines of today prove to be our downfall like Frankenstein's monster?

Science fiction authors try to produce stories showing how man attempts to cope with the problems created by modern technology. But SF can be fun, too – as you will see from these stories. They are drawn from the best of those written in the past 30 years, and we have some new ones, too.

STUART GENDALL

Look, you think you've got troubles

BY CAROL CARR

TO TELL YOU THE TRUTH, in the old days we would have sat shivah for the whole week. My so-called daughter gets married, my own flesh and blood, and not only he doesn't look Jewish, he's not even human.

"Papa," she says to me, two seconds after I refuse to speak to her again in my entire life, "if you know him you'll love him, I promise." So what can I answer – the truth, like I always tell her: "If I know him I'll vomit, that's how he affects me. I can help it? He makes me want to throw up on him."

With silk gloves you have to handle the girl, just like her mother. I tell her what I feel, from the heart, and right away her face collapses into a hundred cracks and water from the Atlantic Ocean makes a soggy mess out of her handkerchief. And that's how I remember her after six months – standing in front of me, sopping wet from the tears and making me feel like a monster – me – when all the time it's her you-should-excuse-the-expression husband who's the monster.

After she's gone to live with him (New Horizon Village, Crag City, Mars), I try to tell myself it's not me who has to – how can I put it? – deal with him intimately; if she can stand it, why should I complain? It's not like I need somebody to carry on the business; my business is to enjoy myself in my retirement. But who can enjoy? Sadie doesn't leave me alone for a minute. She calls me a criminal, a worthless no-good with gallstones for a heart.

"Hector, where's your brains?" she says, having finally given up on my emotions. I can't answer her. I just lost my daughter, I should worry about my brains too? I'm silent as the grave. I can't eat a thing. I'm empty – drained. It's as though I'm waiting for something to happen but I don't know what. I sit in a chair that folds me up like a bee in a flower and rocks me to sleep with electronic rhythms when I feel like sleeping, but who can sleep? I look at my wife and I see Lady Macbeth. Once I caught her whistling as she pushed the button for her bath. I fixed her with a look like an icicle tipped with arsenic.

"What are you so happy about? Thinking of your grandchildren with the 12 toes?"

She doesn't flinch. An iron woman.

When I close my eyes, which is rarely, I see our daughter when she was 14 years old, with skin just beginning to go pimply and no expression yet on her face. I see her walking up to Sadie and asking her what she should do with her life now she's filling out, and my darling Sadie, my life's mate, telling her why not marry a freak; you got to be a beauty to find a man here, but on Mars you shouldn't know from so many fish. "I knew I could count on you, Mama," she says, and goes ahead and marries a plant with legs.

Things go on like this – impossible – for months. I lose 20 lb, my nerves, three teeth and I'm on the verge of losing Sadie, when one day the mailchute goes ding-dong and it's a letter from my late daughter. I take it by the tips of two fingers and bring it in to where my wife is punching ingredients for the gravy I won't eat tonight.

"It's a communication from one of your relatives."

"Oh-oh-oh." My wife makes a grab for it, meanwhile punching CREAM-TOMATO-SAUCE-BEEF DRIPPINGS. No wonder I have no appetite.

"I'll give it to you on one condition only," I tell her, holding it out of her trembling reach. "Take it into the bedroom and read it to yourself. Don't even move your lips for once; I don't want to know. If she's God forbid dead, I'll send him a sympathy card."

Sadie has a variety of expressions but the one thing they have in common is they all wish me misfortune in my present and future life.

While she's reading the letter I find suddenly I have nothing to do. The magazines I read already. Breakfast I ate (like a bird). I'm all dressed to go out if I felt like, but there's nothing outside I don't have inside. Frankly, I don't feel like myself – I'm nervous. I say a lot of things I don't really intend and now maybe this letter comes to tell me I've got to pay for my meanness. Maybe she got sick up there; God knows what they eat, the kind of water they drink, the creatures they run around with. Not wanting to think about it too much, I go over to my chair and turn it on to brisk massage. It doesn't take long till I'm dreaming (fitfully).

I'm someplace surrounded by sand, sitting in a baby's crib and bouncing a diapered kangaroo on my knee. It gurgles up at me and calls me grandpa and I don't know what I should do. I don't want to hurt its feelings, but if I'm a grandpa to a kangaroo, I want no part of it; I only want it should go away. I pull out a coin from my pocket and put it into its pouch. The pouch is full of tiny insects which bite my fingers. I wake up in a sweat.

"Sadie! Are you reading, or rearranging the sentences? Bring it in here and I'll see what she wants. If it's a divorce, I know a lawyer."

Sadie comes into the room with her I-told-you-so waddle and gives me a small wet kiss on the cheek – a gold star for acting like a schmuck. So I start to read it, in a loud monotone so she shouldn't get the impression I give a damn:

"Dear Daddy, I'm sorry for not writing sooner. I suppose I wanted to give you a chance to simmer down first." (Ingrate! Does the sun simmer down?) *"I know it would have been inconvenient for you to come to the wedding, but Mor and I hoped you would maybe send us a letter just to let us know you're okay and still love me, in spite of everything."*

Right at this point I feel a hot sigh followed by a short but wrenching moan.

"Sadie, get away from my neck. I'm warning you . . ."

Her eyes are going flick-a-fleck over my shoulder, from the piece of paper I'm holding to my face, back to the page, flick-a-fleck, flick-a-fleck.

"All right, already," she shoo-shoos me. "I read it, I know what's in it. Now it's your turn to see what kind of a lousy father you turned out to be." And she waddles back into the bedroom, shutting the door extra careful, like she's handling a piece of snow-white velvet.

When I'm certain she's gone, I sit myself down on the slab of woven dental floss my wife calls a couch and press a button on the arm that reads SEMI-CL: FELDMAN TO FRIML. The music starts to slither out from the speaker under my left armpit. The right speaker is dead and buried and the long narrow one at the base years ago got drowned from the dog, who to this day hasn't learned to control himself when he hears *Desert Song*.

This time I'm lucky; it's a piece by Feldman that comes on. I continue to read, calmed by the music.

"I might as well get to the point, Papa, because for all I know you're so mad you've ripped up this letter without even reading it. The point is that Mor and I are going to have a baby. Please, please don't throw this into the disintegrator. It's due in July, which gives you over three months to plan the trip up here. We have a lovely house, with a guest room that you and Mama can stay in for as long as you want."

I have to stop here to interject a couple of questions, since my daughter never had a head for logic and it's my strongest point.

First of all, if she were in front of me in person right now I would ask right off what means 'Mor and I are going to have a baby'. Which? Or both? The second thing is, when she refers to it as 'it' is she being literal or just uncertain? And just one more thing and then I'm through for good: Just how lovely can a guest room be that has all the air piped in and you can't even see the sky or take a walk on the grass because there is no grass, only simulated this and substituted that?

All the above notwithstanding, I continue to read:

"By the way, Papa, there's something I'm not sure you understand. Mor, you may or may not know, is as human as you and me, in all the important ways – and frankly a bit more intelligent."

I put down the letter for a minute just to give the goosebumps a chance to fly out of my stomach ulcers before I go on with her love and best and kisses and hopes for seeing us soon, Lorinda.

I don't know how she manages it, but the second I'm finished, Sadie is out of the bedroom and breathing hard.

"Well, do I start packing or do I start packing? And when I start packing, do I pack for us or do I pack for me?"

"Never. I should die three thousand deaths, each one with a worse prognosis."

* * *

It's a shame a company like Interplanetary Aviation can't afford, with the fares they charge, to give you a comfortable seat. Don't ask how I ever got there in the first place. Ask my wife – she's the one with the mouth. First of all, they only allow you 3 lb of luggage, which if you're only bringing clothes is plenty, but we had a few gifts with us. We were only planning to stay a few days and to sublet the house was Sadie's idea, not mine.

The whole trip was supposed to take a month, each way. This is one reason Sadie thought it was impractical to stay for the weekend and then go home, which was the condition on which I'd agreed to go.

But now that we're on our way, I decide I might as well relax. I close my eyes and try to think of what the first meeting will be like.

"How." I put up my right hand in a gesture of friendship and trust. I reach into my pocket and offer him beads.

But even in my mind he looks at me blank, his naked pink antennae waving in the breeze like a worm's underwear. Then I realise there isn't any breeze where we're going. So they stop waving and wilt.

I look around in my mind. We're alone, the two of us, in the middle of a vast plain, me in my business suit and him in his green skin. The scene looks familiar, like something I had experienced, or read about . . . "We'll meet at Philippi," I think, and stab him with my sword.

Only then am I able to catch a few winks.

The month goes by. When I begin to think I'll never remember how to use a fork, the loudspeaker is turned on and I hear this very smooth, modulated voice, the tranquillised tones of a psychiatrist sucking glycerine, telling us it's just about over, and we should expect a slight jolt upon landing.

The slight jolt starts my life going by so fast I'm missing all the good parts. But finally the ship is still and all you can hear are the wheezes and sighs of the engines – the sounds remind me of Sadie when she's winding down from a good argument. I look around. Everybody is very white. Sadie's five fingers are around my upper arm like a tourniquet.

"We're here," I tell her. "Do I get a hacksaw or can you manage it yourself?"

"Oh, my goodness." She loosens her grip. She really looks a mess – completely pale, not blinking, not even nagging.

I take her by the arm and steer her into customs. All the time I feel that she's a big piece of unwilling luggage I'm smuggling in. There's no co-operation at all in her feet and her eyes are going every which way.

"Sadie, shape up!"

"If you had a little more curiosity about the world you'd be a better person," she says tolerantly.

While we're waiting to be processed by a creature in a suit like ours who surprises me by talking English, I sneak a quick look around.

It's funny. If I didn't know where we are I'd think we're on our lawn. The ground stretches out pure green, and it's only from the leaflet they give you in the ship to keep your mind off the panic that I know it's 100 per cent Acrispan we're looking at, not grass. The air we're getting smells good, too, like fresh-cut flowers, but not too sweet.

By the time I've had a good look and a breathe, what's-its-name is handing us back our passports with a button that says to keep Mars beautiful don't litter.

I won't tell you about the troubles we had getting to the house, or the misunderstanding about the tip, because to be honest I wasn't paying attention. But we do manage to make it to the right door, and considering that the visit was a surprise, I didn't really expect they would meet us at the airport. My daughter must have been peeking, though, because she's in front of us even before we have a chance to knock.

"Mother!" she says, looking very round in the stomach. She hugs and kisses Sadie, who starts bawling. Five minutes later, when they're out of the clinch, Lorinda turns to me, a little nervous.

You can say a lot of things about me, but basically I'm a warm person, and we're about to be guests in this house, even if she is a stranger to me. I shake her hand.

"Is he home, or is he out in the back yard, growing new leaves?"

Her face (or what I can see of it through the climate adapter) crumples a little at the chin line, but she straightens it out and puts her hand on my shoulder.

"Mor had to go out, Daddy – something important came up – but he should be back in an hour or so. Come on, let's go inside."

Actually there's nothing too crazy about the house, or even interesting. It has walls, a floor and a roof, I'm glad to see, even a few relaxer chairs, and after the trip we just had, I sit down and relax. I notice my daughter is having a little trouble looking me straight in the face, which is only as it should be, and it isn't long before she and Sadie are discussing pregnancy, gravitational exercises, labour, hospitals, formulas and sleep-taught toilet training. When I'm starting to feel that I'm getting over-educated, I decide to go into the kitchen and make myself a bite to eat.

I could have asked them for a little something but I don't want to interfere with their first conversation. Sadie has all engines going and is interrupting four times a sentence, which is exactly the kind of game they always had back home – my daughter's goal is to say one complete thought out loud. If Sadie doesn't spring back with a *non sequitur*, Lorinda wins that round. A full-fledged knockout with Sadie still champion is when my daughter can't get a sentence in for a week. Sometimes I can understand why she went to Mars.

Anyway, while they're at the height of their simultaneous monologues, I go quietly off to the kitchen to see what I can dig up. (Ripe parts of Mor, wrapped in plastic? Does he really regenerate, I wonder. Does Lorinda fully understand how he works, or one day will she make an asparagus omelet out of one of his appendages, only to learn that's the part that doesn't grow back? "Oh, I'm so *sorry*," she says. "Can you ever forgive me?")

The refrigerator, though obsolete on Earth, is well stocked – fruits of a sort, steaks, it seems, small chicken-type things that might be stunted pigeons. There's a bowl of a brownish, creamy mess – I can't even bring myself to smell it. Who's hungry, anyway, I think. The rumbling in my stomach is the symptom of a father's love turning sour.

I wander into the bedroom. There's a large portrait of Mor hanging on the wall – or maybe his ancestor. Is it true that instead of hearts, Martians have a large avocado pit? There's a rumour on Earth that when Martians get old they start to turn brown at the edges, like lettuce.

There's an object on the floor and I bend down and pick it up. A piece of material – at home I would have thought it was a man's handkerchief. Maybe it is a handkerchief. Maybe they have colds like us. They catch a germ, the sap rises to combat the infection, and they have to blow their stamens. I open up a drawer to put the piece of material in (I like to be neat), but when I close it, something gets stuck. Another thing I can't recognise. It's small, round and either concave or convex, depending on how you look at it. It's made of something black and shiny. A skullcap? What would a vegetable be doing with a skullcap? Some questions are too deep for me, but what I don't know I eventually find out – and not by asking, either.

I go back to the living-room.

"Did you find anything to eat?" Lorinda asks. "Or would you like me to fix . . .?"

"Don't even get up," Sadie says quickly. "I can find my way around any kitchen, I don't care whose."

"I'm not hungry. It was a terrible trip. I thought I'd never wake up from it in one piece. By the way, I heard a good riddle on the ship. What's round and black, either concave or convex, depending on how you look at it, and made out of a shiny material?"

Lorinda blushed. "A skullcap? But that's not funny."

"So who needs funny? Riddles have to be a laugh a minute all of a sudden? You think Oedipus giggled all the way home from seeing the Sphinx?"

"Look, Daddy, I think there's something I should tell you."

"I think there are all sorts of things you should tell me."

"No, I mean about Mor."

"Who do you think *I* mean, the grocery boy? You elope with a cucumber from outer space and you want I should be satisfied because he's human in all the important ways? What's important – that he sneezes and hiccups? If you tell me he snores, I should be ecstatic?

Maybe he sneezes when he's happy and hiccups when he's making love and snores because it helps him think better. Does that make him human?"

"Daddy, *please*."

"Okay, not another word." Actually I'm starting to feel quite guilty. What if she has a miscarriage right on the spot? A man like me doesn't blithely torture a pregnant woman, even if she does happen to be his daughter. "What's so important it can't wait till later?"

"Nothing, I guess. Would you like some chopped liver? I just made some fresh."

"What?"

"Chopped liver – you know, chopped liver."

Oh yes, the ugly mess in the refrigerator. "You made it, that stuff in the bowl?"

"Sure. Daddy, there's something I really have to tell you."

She never does get to tell me, though, because her husband walks in, bold as brass.

I won't even begin to tell you what he looks like. Let me just say he's a good dream cooked up by Mary Shelley. I won't go into it, but if it gives you a small idea, I'll say that his head is shaped like an acorn on top of a stalk of broccoli. Enormous blue eyes, green skin and no hair at all except for a small blue round area on top of his head. His ears are adorable. Remember Dumbo the Elephant? Only a little smaller – I never exaggerate, even for effect. And he looks boneless, like a fillet.

My wife, God bless her, I don't have to worry about; she's a gem in a crisis. One look at her son-in-law and she faints dead away. If I didn't know her better, if I wasn't absolutely certain that her simple mind contained no guile, I would have sworn she did it on purpose, to give everybody something to fuss about. Before we know what's happening, we're all in a tight, frantic conversation about what's the best way to bring her around. But while my daughter and her husband are in the bathroom looking for some deadly chemical, Sadie opens both eyes at once and stares up at me from the floor.

"What did I miss?"

"You didn't miss anything – you were only unconscious for 15 seconds. It was a cat nap, not a coma."

"Say hello, Hector. Say hello to him or so help me I'll close my eyes for good."

"I'm very glad to meet you, Mr. Trumbnick," he says. I'm grateful that he's sparing me the humiliation of making the first gesture, but I pretend I don't see the stalk he's holding out.

"Smutual," I say.

"I beg your pardon?"

"Smutual. How are you? You look better than your pictures." He does too. Even though his skin is green, it looks like the real thing up close. But his top lip sort of vibrates when he talks, and I can hardly bear to look at him except sideways.

"I hear you had some business this afternoon. My daughter never did tell me what your line is, uh, Morton."

"Daddy, his name is Mor. Why don't you call him Mor?"

"Because I prefer Morton. When we know each other better I'll call him something less formal. Don't rush me, Lorinda; I'm still getting adjusted to the chopped liver."

My son-in-law chuckles and his top lip really goes crazy. "Oh, were you surprised? Imported meats aren't a rarity here, you know. Just the other day one of my clients was telling me about an all-Earth meal he had at home."

"Your client?" Sadie asks. "You wouldn't happen to be a lawyer?" (My wife amazes me with her instant familiarity. She could live with a *Tyrannosaurus* in perfect harmony. First she faints, and while she's out cold everything in her head that was strange becomes ordinary and she wakes up a new woman.)

"No, Mrs. Trumbnick. I'm a . . ."

". . . rabbi, of course," she finishes. "I knew it. The minute Hector found that skullcap I knew it. Him and his riddles. A skullcap is a skullcap and nobody not Jewish would dare wear one – not even a Martian." She bites her lip but recovers like a pro. "I'll bet you were out on a Bar Mitzvah – right?"

"No, as a matter of fact . . ."

". . . a Bris. I knew it."

She's rubbing her hands together and beaming at him. "A Bris, how *nice*. But why didn't you tell us, Lorinda? Why would you keep such a thing a secret?"

Lorinda comes over to me and kisses me on the cheek, and I wish she wouldn't because I'm feeling myself go soft and I don't want to show it.

"Mor isn't *just* a rabbi, Daddy. He converted because of me and then found there was a demand among the colonists. But he's never given up his own beliefs, and part of his job is to minister to the Kopchopees who camp outside the village. That's where he was earlier, conducting a Kopchopee menopausal rite."

"A what!"

"Look, to each his own," says my wife with the open mind. But me, I want facts, and this is getting more bizarre by the minute.

"Kopchopee. He's a Kopchopee priest to his own race and a rabbi to ours, and that's how he makes his living? You don't feel there's a contradiction between the two, Morton?"

"That's right. They both pray to a strong silent god, in different ways of course. The way my race worships, for instance . . ."

"Listen, it takes all kinds," says Sadie.

"And the baby, whatever it turns out to be – will it be a Choptapi or a Jew?"

"Jew, shmoo," Sadie says with a wave of dismissal. "All of a sudden it's Hector the Pious – such a mountain out of a molehill." She turns away from me and addresses herself to the others, like I've just become invisible. "He hasn't seen the inside of a synagogue since we got married – what a rain that night – and now he can't take his shoes off in a house until he knows its race, colour and creed." With a face full of fury, she brings me back into her sight. "Idiot, what's got into you?"

I stand up straight to preserve my dignity. "If you'll excuse me, my things are getting wrinkled in the suitcase."

Sitting on my bed (with shoes on), I must admit I'm feeling a little different. Not that Sadie made me change my mind. Far from it; for many years now her voice is the white sound that lets me think my own thoughts. But what I'm realising more and more is that in a situation like this a girl needs her father, and what kind of a man is it who can't sacrifice his personal feelings for his only daughter? When she was going out with Herbie the Haemopheliac and came home crying it had to end because she was afraid to touch him, he might bleed, didn't I say pack your things, we're going to Grossingers Venus for three weeks?

When my twin brother Max went into kitchen sinks, who was it that helped him out at only four per cent? Always, I stood ready to help my family. And if Lorinda ever needed me, it's now when she's pregnant by some religious maniac. Okay – he makes me retch, so I'll talk to him with a tissue over my mouth. After all, in a world that's getting smaller all the time, it's people like me who have to be bigger to make up for it, no?

I go back to the living-room and extend my hand to my son-in-law the cauliflower. (Feh.)

Security

BY BRIAN M. STABLEFORD

THE NEW D.H.S.S. BUILDING was fitted with the largest solar-powered air-conditioning system in London. The day Hatherley called, something had gone wrong with the automatic control-unit and crossing the threshold felt rather like stepping out of a plane in Nairobi. As the lift took him up to the 32nd floor he hoped that the corridors might be cooler at high altitude, but it proved to be a forlorn hope.

He was shown into Eldon's office by a slightly-overweight receptionist whose make-up had been hastily repaired during a recent tea-break. Eldon was the first person he had seen in the building who seemed completely unaffected by the tropical atmosphere.

"Delighted to see you," murmured Eldon, seizing his hand with a practised grip. "Know your work, of course. Three of our secretarial executives trained in your department. Lifeblood of the nation today, computer studies. Where would we be without first-class software in today's world?"

Hatherley resisted the temptation to provide a suitably expressive answer, and allowed Eldon to propel him gently into a leather-clad chair. The ministerial assistant's solicitous over-friendliness disappeared as he took up his own position, as if the relationship between them had altered at the flick of a switch. "Now," said Eldon, "I'm afraid you'll have to forgive me for being blunt, professor, but I have another appointment at 12.

"Ordinarily, we don't grant interviews like this at all, but your letter was so unusual that we made an exception. I'm not at all sure that I have this straight, but it seems that you're asking us to authorise social security payments to a computer."

There was only the ghost of a smile on Hatherley's lips as he said: "That's correct." He didn't like the use of the word "computer" in this context, but had learned that there was no point in arguing about it. He hoped that Eldon wouldn't make any jokes about computers paying out social security but not collecting it. He needn't have worried – Eldon never joked. He had no sense of humour.

"Would you care to explain?" invited the ministerial assistant.

Hatherley took a deep breath. "The background detail is filled out in the letter," he said. "My team is one of several that began work in the early 1980s on projects to develop a new kind of artificial intelligence – the provision of machines with self-modifying programs that would give them the means to think in abstract terms, as humans do. Our hardware was provided by groups in California and Paris, where they've gone much further than we have in developing sensory apparatus for use with the present generation of artificial intelligences. What we were aiming to do, in the simplest possible terms, was to produce a self-aware consciousness capable of all the modes of thought we consider to be typically human.

"Several of the projects have been successful, and you've no doubt been distracted from the importance of the discovery by the battle to establish priority that has been covered more than adequately in the Press. As far as we can tell, Max didn't win the race, but that's not really important by comparison with the main issue."

"Max, of course, is your sentient machine," said Eldon. "What do the letters stand for?"

"They don't stand for anything," said Hatherley. "Max is his *name*, not a shorthand version of some ponderously clever label."

Eldon looked mildly surprised by the rebuke.

"In a sense," Hatherley went on, "my work with Max is already complete. All the theoretical problems I set out to solve in building him are pretty well sorted out. I'm now ready to start on a new machine, which will be intellectually more capable. That's not to say that Max has stopped developing his abilities and his personality – just that what I've learned from him can now be put to better use in starting again from scratch. My . . . *parental* responsibilities towards Max are virtually at an end.

"It's time for him to take charge of his own destiny – if he's allowed to. That's why I'm here. It's not the money, you understand – what I'm really after is recognition of Max as a person."

Eldon was watching him with a kind of wary stare that Hatherley had seen before, suggestive of slight doubts as to his sanity. Most people expected scientists to be out of touch with reality.

I'm afraid I *don't* understand," said Eldon.

"It's simple enough," Hatherley assured him. "I'm trying to secure for Max the same legal rights that any other person has. I'm trying to establish that switching him off would constitute murder, and that tampering with his programming without his consent would constitute a serious infringement of his right of self-determination."

"I don't see what it has to do with us," said Eldon.

"Sooner or later," explained the professor, patiently, "this is likely to come to court. At present, Max and his kindred are safe. They don't pose any threat to anyone. But they're the first of a *new* race, and there are people who consider them to be potentially dangerous. At some stage, it will have to be decided what rights these new beings have, and what responsibilities *we* have towards them. I'm trying to establish for Max a degree of legal protection *before* the argument gets bogged down in a morass of hysterical fears and horror stories.

"It would aid my case considerably if a government department like yours were to concede implicit recognition of Max's rights as an individual. That's why I'm applying to you on his behalf for some contribution towards his upkeep. He occupies space in a university laboratory, which has to be rented. He has to be kept in good order, in a carefully-controlled environment. He also maintains telephonic contact with other machines, including two of his kin."

"Doesn't the university pay for all this?" asked Eldon.

"At present. Some of the money originates from public funds, the rest comes initially from the private sponsors who have given grant support to my work."

"In that case," said Eldon. "He's not actually in *need*. Even if he *were* a person – and I think you'd have to settle that in court before we could consider any kind of application – I don't see that he'd be eligible for any kind of financial assistance from us. I don't see that we could involve ourselves on any grounds whatever."

"You might give him a social security number," said Hatherley, patiently. "You could make him a statistic in your computer storage systems. That's all it takes to be a person, these days – isn't it?"

"I'm afraid you're putting the cart before the horse," said Eldon, with equal patience. "If the courts will recognise Max as a person, we'll be pleased to allocate him a social security number. Until then, it's out of the question. We couldn't possibly be seen to be pre-empting the decision of the courts."

"We need help," said Hatherley. "We need help from anywhere we can get it. It isn't going to be easy to fight the case for Max's humanity. But it has to be fought. The university is willing to give Max a contract, by which he becomes an employee rather than an experimental object. They can't do that, though, unless your department will take him on to your books.

"Someone, somewhere, has to make the first move. Max is patient, of course – after all, if things *do* work out in his favour he's potentially immortal – but I believe that now is the time to get things done."

"I'll refer the matter to the Minister, if you insist," said Eldon, woodenly. "I can't hold out much hope, though."

Hatherley stood up. "I thought that it was worth a try," he said. "It would have been a great help to us to receive some kind of implicit recognition for Max. I didn't really think that it would work. Still, as Max said only yesterday, when his kind get their turn, they probably won't treat *us* so very much better."

As Eldon moved around his desk in order to show the professor to the door his officious personality dropped from him like a cloak, and the air of mechanical efficiency was replaced by one of casual *bonhomie*. He smiled as he said: "Too subtle for me, I fear. I can't quite see the joke."

"No," said Hatherley. "But *he* can."

I, Mars

BY RAY BRADBURY

THE PHONE RANG. A grey hand lifted the receiver.

"Hello."

"Hello, Barton?"

"Yes."

"This is Barton."

"What?"

"This is Barton!"

"It can't be. This phone hasn't rung in 20 years."

The old man hung up.

Brrrrinnnng!

His grey hand seized the phone.

"Hello, Barton," laughed the voice. "You have forgotten, haven't you?"

The old man felt his heart grow small and like a cool stone. He felt the wind blowing in off the dry seas and the blue hills of Mars. After 20 years of silence and cobwebs and now, tonight, on his 80th birthday, with a ghastly scream, this phone had wailed to life.

"Who did you think it was?" said the voice. "A rocket captain? Did you think someone had come to rescue you?"

"No."

"What's the date?"

Numbly, "July 20, 2097."

"Good Lord. Sixty years! Have you been sitting there that long? Waiting for a rocket to come from Earth to rescue you?"

The old man nodded.

"Now, old man, do you know who I am?"

"Yes." The dry pale lips trembling. "I understand. I remember. I am Emil Barton and you are Emil Barton."

"With one difference. You are 80. I am only 20. All of life before me!"

The old man began to laugh and then to cry. He sat holding the phone like a lost child. The conversation was impossible, and should not be continued, and yet he went on with it. When he got hold of himself he held the phone close to his withered lips and said, in deepest anguish: "Listen! You there! Listen, oh God, if I could warn you! How can I? You're only a voice. If I could show you how lonely the years are. End it, kill yourself! Don't wait! If you knew what it is to change from the thing you are to the thing that is me, today, here, now, at this end."

"Impossible." The voice of the young Barton laughed, far away. "I've no way to tell if you ever get this call. You're talking to a transcription. This is 2037. Sixty years in your past. Today, the atomic war started on Earth. All colonials were called home from Mars, by rocket. I got left behind!"

"I remember," whispered the old man.

"Alone on Mars," laughed the young voice. "A month, a year, who cares? There are books and food. In my spare time I've made transcription libraries of 10,000 words, responses, my voice, connected to phone relays. In later months I'll call, have somebody to talk with."

"Yes," murmured the old man, remembering.

"My own transcripto-tapes will ring me up 60 years from now. I don't really think I'll be here on Mars that long; it's just a beautifully ironic idea of mine, something to pass the time. Is that really you, Barton? Is that really me?"

Tears fell from the old man's eyes. "Yes!"

"I've made a thousand Bartons, tapes, sensitive to all questions, my voice, in a thousand Martian towns. An army of Bartons over Mars, while I wait for the rockets to return."

"You fool," the old man shook his head, wearily. "You waited 60 years. You grew old waiting, always alone. And now you've become me and you're still alone in the empty cities."

"Don't expect my sympathy. You're like a stranger, off in another

RAY BRADBURY

CONSIDERED by many readers and critics to be "the poet of science fiction", Ray Douglas Bradbury writes with a highly emotional and stylized prose.

Born in 1920 in Illinois he showed an early interest in fantasy fiction particularly the stories of Edgar Allen Poe. He began writing at the age of 12 and at 21 had his first story, a collaboration with Henry Hasse, published by *Super-Science Stories*.

The poetic fantasy *The Martian Chronicles* is a collection of his short stories from the 1940's. Loosely interconnected they form a disturbing glimpse of an attempted colonization of Mars and the destruction of its once great Martian civilization. The most powerful piece in the book is *And the Moon be still as bright*.

The series were recently adapted for television and shown in Britain.

In 1966 Francois Truffaut directed a film of Bradbury's *Fahrenheit 451* an anti-utopian novel which tells the story of Montague a fire-man whose job it is to burn books.

A complete all-rounder, Bradbury has lectured on creative writing, poetry and architecture. He designed the American Pavilion at the 1964 New York World's Fair. He is currently concentrating on adapting some of his work for the stage, and on his poetry.

***I, Mars* is a frightening portrait of a man's struggle to remain sane after being abandoned on Mars.**

country. I can't be sad. I'm alive when I make these tapes. And you're alive when you hear them. Both of us, to the other, incomprehensible. Neither can warn the other, even though both respond, one to the other, one automatically, the other warmly and humanly. I'm human now. You're human later. I can't cry, because not knowing the future I can only be optimistic. These hidden tapes can only react to a certain number of stimuli from you. Can you ask a dead man to weep?"

"Stop it!" cried the old man. He felt the familiar great seizures of pain. Nausea moved through him, and blackness. "Stop it! Oh God, but you were heartless. Go away!"

"Were, old man? I *am*. As long as the tapes glide on, as long as secret spindles and hidden electronic eyes read and select and convert words to send to you, I'll be young, cruel, blunt. I'll go on being young and cruel long after you're dead. Good-bye."

Click.

* * *

Barton sat holding the silent phone a long while. His heart gave him intense pain.

What insanity it had been, in those first secluded years, fixing the telephonic brains, the tapes, the circuits, scheduling calls on time relays:

Brrrrinnnng!

"Morning, Barton. This is Barton. Seven o'clock. Rise and shine!"

Brrrrinnnng!

"Barton calling. You're to go to Mars Town at noon. Install a telephonic brain. Thought I'd remind you."

"Thanks."

Brrrrinnnng!

"Barton? Barton. Have lunch with me? The Rocket Inn?"

"Right."

Brrrrinnnng!

"Thank you, B.? Thought I'd cheer you. Firm chin, and all that. The rescue rocket might come tomorrow, to save you."

"Yes, tomorrow, tomorrow, tomorrow, tomorrow."

Click.

But 40 years had burned into smoke. Barton had muted the insidious phones and their clever, clever repartee. He had sealed them into silences. They were to call him only after he was 80, if he still lived. And now today, the phones ringing, and the past was breathing in his ear, sighing, whispering, murmuring, and remembering.

Brrrrinnnng!

He let it ring.

"I don't have to answer it," he thought.

Brrrrinnnng!

"There's no one there at all," he thought.

Brrrrinnnng!

"It's like talking to yourself," he thought. "But different. Oh God, how different."

He felt his hands crawl unconsciously towards the phone.

Click.

"Hello, old Barton, this is young Barton. One year older, though. I'm 21 today. In the last year I've put voice brains in 200 towns on Mars. I've populated it with arrogant Bartons!"

"Yes." The old man remembered those days six decades ago, those nights of rushing over blue hills and into iron valleys of Mars, with a truckful of machinery, whistling, happy. Another telephone, another relay. Something to do. Something clever and wonderful and sad. Hidden voices. Hidden, hidden. In those young days when death was not death, time was not time, old age a faint echo from the long blue cavern of years ahead. That young idiot, that sadistic fool, never thinking to reap the harvest so sown.

"Last night," said Barton, aged 21, "I sat alone in a movie theatre in an empty town. I played an old Laurel and Hardy. God, how I laughed."

"Yes."

"I got an idea today. I recorded my voice 1,000 times on tape. Broadcast from the town, it sounds like 1,000 people living there. A comforting noise, the noise of a crowd. I fixed it so doors slam in town, children sing, music boxes play, all by clockwork. If I don't look out of the window, if I just listen, it's all right. But if I look, it spoils the illusion. I guess I'm getting lonely."

The old man said, "Yes. That was your first sign."

"What?"

"The first time you admitted you were lonely."

"I've experimented with smells. As I walk down the deserted streets, the smells of bacon and eggs, ham steak, filets, soups, come from the houses. All done with hidden machines. Clever?"

"Fantasy. Madness."

"Self-protection, old man."

"I'm tired." Abruptly the old man hung up. It was too much. The past pouring over him, drowning him . . .

Swaying, he moved down the tower stairs to the streets of the town.

The town was dark. No longer did red neons burn, music play, or cooking smells linger. Long ago he had abandoned the grim fantasy of the mechanical lie. Listen! Are those footsteps? Smell! Isn't that strawberry pie? No, he had stopped it all. What had he done with the robots? His mind puzzled. Oh yes . . .

He moved to the dark canal where the stars shone in the quivering waters.

Underwater, in row after fish-like row, rusting, were the robot population of Mars he had constructed over the years, and, in a wild realisation of his own insane inadequacy, had commanded to march, one-two-three-four! into the canal deeps, plunging, bubbling like sunken bottles. He had killed then and shown no remorse.

* * *

Brrrrinnnng.

Faintly a phone rang in a lightless cottage.

He walked on. The phone ceased.

Brrrrinnnng. Another cottage ahead, as if it knew of his passing. He began to run. The ringing stayed behind. Only to be taken up by a ringing from now this house – *Brrrrinnnng!* now that, now here, there! He turned the corner. A phone! He darted on. Another corner. Another phone!

"All right, all right!" he shrieked, exhausted. "I'm coming!"

"Hello, Barton."

"What do you want!"

"I'm lonely. I only live when I speak. So I must speak. You can't shut me up forever."

"Leave me alone!" said the old man, in horror.

"This is Barton, age 24. Another couple of years gone. Waiting. A little lonelier. I've read *War and Peace*, drunk sherry, run restaurants with myself as waiter, cook, entertainer. And tonight, I star in a film at the Tivoli. Emil Barton in *Love's Labour Lost*, playing all the parts, some with wigs, myself!"

"Stop calling me," the old man's eyes were fiery and insane. "Or I'll kill you!"

"You can't kill me. You'll have to find me, first!"

"I'll find you!" A choking.

"You've forgotten where you hid me. I'm everywhere in Mars, in boxes, in houses, in cables, towers, underground! Go ahead, try! What'll you call it? Telecide? Suicide? Jealous, are you? Jealous of me here, only 24, bright-eyed, strong, young, young, young? All right, old man, it's war! Between us. Between me! A whole regiment of us, all ages from 20 to 60, against you, the real one. Go ahead, declare war!"

"I'll kill you!" screamed Barton.

Click. Silence.

"Kill you!" He threw the phone out of the window, shrieking.

* * *

In the midnight cold, the ancient automobile moved in deep valleys. Under Barton's feet on the floorboard were revolvers, rifles, dynamite. The roar of the car was in his thin, tired bones.

I'll find them, he thought. Find and destory, all of them. Oh, God, God, how can he do this to me?

He stopped the car. A strange town lay under the late twin moons. There was no wind.

He held the rifle in his cold hands. He peered at the poles, the towers, the boxes. Where? Where was this town's voice hidden? That tower? Or that one there! Where! So many years ago. So long gone. So forgotten. He turned his head now this way, now that, wildly. It must be that tower! Was he certain? Or this box here, or the transformer half up that tower?

He raised the rifle.

The tower fell with the first bullet.

All of them, he thought. All of the towers in this town will have to be cut apart. I've forgotten. Too long.

The car moved along the silent street.

Brrrrinnnng!

He looked at the deserted bar.

Brrrrinnnng!

Pistol in hand, he entered.

Click.

"Hello, Barton? Just a warning. Don't try to rip down all the towers, blow things up. Cut your own throat that way. Think it over . . ."

Click.

He stepped out of the phone booth slowly and moved into the street and listened to the telephone towers humming high in the air, still alive, still untouched. He looked at them and then he understood.

He could not destroy the towers. Suppose a rocket came from Earth, impossible idea, but suppose it came tonight, tomorrow, next week? And landed on the other side of the planet, and used the phones to try to call Barton, only to find the circuits dead?

Barton dropped his gun.

"A rocket won't come," he argued, softly, logically with himself. "I'm old. It won't come now. It's too late."

But suppose it came, and you never knew, he thought. No, you've got to keep the lines open.

Brrrrinnnng.

* * *

He turned dully. His eyes were blinking and not seeing. He shuffled back into the bar and fumbled with the receiver.

"Hello?" A strange voice.

"Please," pleaded the old man, brokenly. "Don't bother me."

"Who's this, who's there? *Who* is it? Where are you?" cried the voice, surprised.

"Wait a minute." The old man staggered. "This is Emil Barton, who's that?"

"This is Captain Leonard Rockwell, Earth Rocket 48. Just arrived from New York."

"No, no, no."

"Are you there, Mr. Barton?"

"No, no, it can't be, it just can't."

"Where are you?"

"You're lying, it's false!" The old man had to lean against the booth wall. His blue eyes were cold blind. "It's you, Barton, making fun of me, lying to me again!"

"This is Captain Rockwell. We just landed in New Schenectady. Where are you?"

"In Green Town," he gasped. "That's 1,000 miles from you."

"Look, Barton, can you come here?"
"What?"
"We've repairs on our rocket. Exhausted from the flight. Can you help?"
"Yes, yes."
"We're on the tarmac outside town. Can you reach us by tomorrow."
"Yes, but . . ."
"Well?"
The old man caressed the phone, pitifully. "How's Earth? How's New York? Is the war over? Who's President now? What happened?"
"Plenty of time for gossip when you arrive."
"Is everything fine?"
"Fine."
"Thank God." The old man listened to the far voice. "Are you sure you're Captain Rockwell?"
"Damn it, man!"
"I'm sorry!"
He hung up and ran.
They were here, after so many years, unbelievable, his own, who would take him back to Earth seas and skies and mountains.
He started the car. He would drive all night. Could he do it? What of his heart – It would be worth a risk, to see people, to shake hands, to hear them near you.
The car thundered in the hills.
That voice. Captain Rockwell. It couldn't be himself, 40 years ago. He had never made a recording like that. Or had he? In one of his depressive fits, in a spell of drunken cynicism, hadn't he once made a false tape of a false landing on Mars with a synthetic captain, an imaginary crew? He jerked his grey head, savagely. No. He was a suspicious fool. Now was not time to doubt. He must run under the moons of Mars, hour on hour. What a party they would have!
The sun rose. He was immensely tired, full of thorns and brambles of weakness, his heart plunging and aching, his fingers fumbling the wheel, but the thing that pleased him most was the thought of one last phone call: Hello, young Barton, this is old Barton. I'm leaving for Earth today! Rescued! He chuckled weakly.
He drove into the shadowy limits of New Schenectady at sunset. Stepping from his car he stood staring at the rocket tarmac, rubbing his reddened eyes.
The rocket field was empty. No one ran to meet him. No one shook his hand, shouted, or laughed.
He felt his heart roar into pain. He knew blackness and a sensation of falling through the open sky. He stumbled towards an office.
Inside, six phones sat in a neat row.
He waited, gasping.
Finally:
Brrrrinnnng.
He lifted the heavy receiver.

A voice said, "I was wondering if you'd get there alive."

The old man did not speak, but stood with the phone in his hands.

The voice continued, "An elaborate joke. Captain Rockwell reporting for duty, sir. Your orders, sir?"

"You," groaned the old man.

"How's your heart, old man?"

"No!"

"Hoped the trip would kill you. Had to eliminate you some way, so I could live, if you call a transcription living."

"I'm going out now," replied the old man, "and blow it all up. I don't care. I'll blow up everything until you're all dead!"

"You haven't the strength. Why do you think I had you travel so far, so fast? This is your last trip!"

The old man felt his heart falter. He would never make the other towns. The war was lost. He slid into a chair and made low sobbing, mournful noises from his loose mouth. He glared at the five other, silent phones. As if at a signal, they burst into silver chorus! A nest of ugly birds screaming!

Automatic receivers popped up.

The office whirled. "Barton, Barton, Barton!!"

He throttled the phone in his hands, the voice, the youth, the time of long ago. He smashed it, choked it and still it laughed at him. He throttled it. He beat it. He kicked at it. He hated it with hands and mouth and blind raging eye. He furled the hot wire like serpentine in his fingers, ripped it into red bits which fell about his stumbling feet.

He destroyed three other phones. There was a sudden silence.

And as if his body now discovered a thing which it had long kept secret, it seemed to decay upon his tired bones. The flesh of his eyelids fell away like flower petals. His mouth became a withered rose. The lobes of his ears melting wax. He pushed his chest with his hands and fell face down. He lay still. His breathing stopped. His heart stopped.

After a long spell, the remaining two phones rang.

Twice. Three times.

A relay snapped somewhere. The two phone voices were connected, one to the other.

"Hello, Barton."

"Yes, Barton?"

"What's happened?"

"I don't know. Listen."

The silent room. The old man did not stir on the floor. The wind blew through the broken window. The air was cool.

"Congratulate me, Barton, this is my 26th birthday!"

"And I'm 24!"

"Congratulations!"

Laughter drifted out the window into the dead city.

Great Lost Discoveries — I

Invisibility

BY FREDRIC BROWN

THREE GREAT DISCOVERIES WERE MADE, and tragically lost, during the 20th-century. The first of these was the secret of invisibility.

The secret of invisibility was discovered in 1909 by Archibald Praeter, emissary from the court of Edward VII to the court of Sultan Abd el Krim, ruler of a small state loosely allied to the Ottoman Empire.

Praeter, an amateur but enthusiastic biologist, was injecting mice with various serums for the purpose of finding an injection which would cause mutations. When he injected his 3,019th mouse, the mouse disappeared. It was still there; he could feel it in his hand, but he could not see a hair or claw of it. He put it carefully in a cage and two hours later it appeared again, unharmed.

He experimented with increasing dosages and found that he could make a mouse invisible for up to 24 hours. Larger doses made it ill or

torpid. He also learned that a mouse killed while invisible reappeared instantly at the moment of death.

Realising the importance of his discovery, he wired his resignation to England, dismissed his servants and locked himself in his quarters, and began to experiment with himself. Starting with a small injection that made him invisible for only a few minutes, he worked up until he found his tolerance was equal to that of mice; an injection that made him invisible for more than 24 hours also made him ill. He also found that although nothing of his body was visible, not even his dentures if he kept his lips closed, nudity was essential, clothing did not become invisible with him.

Praeter was an honest and fairly well-to-do-man, so he did not think of crime. He decided to return to England and offer his discovery to His Majesty's government for use in espionage or war.

But he decided first to allow himself one indulgence. He had always been curious about the closely-guarded harem of the Sultan to whose court he had been attached. Why not have a close look at it from inside?

Besides, something – some nagging thought that he couldn't quite isolate – bothered him about his discovery. There was some circumstance under which . . . He couldn't get beyond that point in his mind. An experiment was definitely in order.

He stripped and made himself invisible for the maximum period. It proved simple to walk past the armed eunuchs and enter the harem. He spent an interesting afternoon watching the 50-odd beauties at their daytime occupation of keeping themselves beautiful, bathing and anointing their bodies with scented oils and perfumes.

One, a Circassian, especially attracted him. It occurred to him, just as it would have occured to any man, that if he stayed the night – perfectly safe since he would be invisible until the following noon – he could keep her in sight to learn which room she slept in and, after the lights were out, join her; she would think the Sultan was favouring her with a visit.

He kept her in sight and noticed the room she entered. An armed eunuch took his post at the curtained doorway, others at each of the other doorways to the sleeping rooms. He waited until he was sure she would be asleep and then, at a moment when the eunuch was looking down the hall and would not see the movement of the curtain, he slipped through it.

The light had been dim in the hallway; here the darkness was utter. But he groped carefully and managed to find the sleeping couch. Carefully he put out a hand and touched the sleeping woman. She screamed. (What he had not known was that the Sultan never visited the harem by night but sent for one, or sometimes several, of his wives to visit his own quarters.)

And suddenly the eunuch who had been outside was inside and had hold of him by the arm. The last thing he thought was that he now knew the one worrisome circumstance of invisibility: it was completely useless in pitch darkness. And the last thing he heard was the swish of the scimitar.

The sixth palace

BY ROBERT SILVERBERG

Ben Azai was deemed worthy and stood at the gate of the sixth palace and saw the ethereal splendour of the pure marble plates. He opened his mouth and said twice, "Water! Water!" In the twinkling of an eye they decapitated him and threw eleven thousand iron bars at him. This shall be a sign for all generations that no one should err at the gate of the sixth palace.

— *Lesser Hekhaloth*

THERE WAS THE TREASURE, and there was the guardian of the treasure. And there were the whitening bones of those who had tried in vain to make the treasure their own. Even the bones had taken on a kind of beauty, lying out there by that gate of the treasure vault, under the blazing arch of heavens. The treasure itself lent beauty to everything near it – even the scattered bones, even the grim guardian.

The home of the treasure was a small world that belonged to red Valzar. Hardly more than moon-sized, really, with no atmosphere to speak of, a silent, dead little world that spun through darkness a billion miles from its cooling primary. A wayfarer had stopped there once. Where from, where bound? No one knew. He had established a cache there, and there it lay, changeless and eternal, treasure beyond belief, presided over by the faceless metal man who waited with metal patience for his master's return.

There were those who would have the treasure. They came, and were challenged by the guardian, and died.

On another world of the Valzar system, men undiscouraged by the fate of their predecessors dreamed of the hoard, and schemed to possess it. Lipescu was one: a tower of a man, golden beard, fists like hammers, gullet of brass, back as broad as a tree of a thousand years. Bolzano was another: awl-shaped, bright of eye, fast of finger, twig thick, razor sharp. They had no wish to die.

Lipescu's voice was like the rumble of island Galaxies in collision. He wrapped himself around a tankard of good black ale and said, "I go tomorrow, Bolzano."

"Is the computer ready?"

"Programmed with everything the beast could ask me," the big man boomed. "There won't be a slip."

"And if there is?" Bolzano asked, peering idly into the blue, oddly pale, strangely meek eyes of the giant. "And if the robot kills you?"

"I've dealt with robots before."

Bolzano laughed. "That plain is littered with bones, friend. Yours will join the rest. Great bulky bones, Lipescu. I can see them now."

"You're a cheerful one, friend."

"I'm realistic."

Lipescu shook his head heavily. "If you were realistic, you wouldn't be in this with me," he said slowly. "Only a dreamer would do such a thing as this." One meaty paw hovered in the air, pounced, caught Bolzano's forearm. The little man winced as bones ground together. Lipescu said, "You won't back out? If I die, you'll make the attempt?"

"Of course I will, you idiot."

"Will you? You're a coward, like all little men. You'll watch me die, and then you'll turn tail and head for another part of the universe as fast as you know how. Won't you?"

"I intend to profit by your mistakes," Bolzano said in a clear, testy voice. "Let go of my arm."

Lipescu released his grip. The little man sank back in his chair, rubbing his arm. He gulped ale. He grinned at his partner and raised his glass.

"To success," Bolzano said.

"Yes. To the treasure."

"And to long life afterwards."

"For both of us," the big man boomed.

"Perhaps," said Bolzano. "Perhaps."

* * *

He had his doubts. The big man was sly, Ferd Bolzano knew, and that was a good combination, not often found: slyness and size. Yet the risks were great. Bolzano wondered which he preferred – that Lipescu should gain the treasure on his attempt, thus assuring Bolzano of a share without risk, or that Lipescu should die, forcing Bolzano to venture his own life. Which was better, a third of the treasure without hazard, or the whole thing for the highest stake?

Bolzano was a good enough gambler to know the answer to that. Yet there was more than yellowness to the man; in his own way, he longed for the chance to risk his life on the airless treasure world.

Lipescu would go first. That was the agreement. Bolzano had stolen the computer, had turned it over to the big man, and Lipescu would make the initial attempt. If he gained the prize, his was the greater share. If he perished, it was Bolzano's moment next. An odd partnership, odd terms, but Lipescu would have it no other way, and Ferd Bolzano did not argue the point with his beefy compatriot. Lipescu would return with the treasure, or he would not return at all. There would be no middle way, they both were certain.

Bolzano spent an uneasy night. His apartment, in an airy shaft of a building overlooking the glittering Lake Eris, was a comfortable place, and he had little longing to leave it. Lipescu, by preference, lived in the stinking slums beyond the southern shore of the lake, and when the two men parted for the night they went in opposite ways. Bolzano considered bringing a woman home for the night but did not.

Instead, he sat moody and wakeful before the televector screen, watching the procession of worlds, peering at the green and gold and ochre planets as they sailed through the emptiness.

Towards dawn, he ran the tape of the treasure. Octave Merlin had made that tape, 100 years before, as he orbited 60 miles above the surface of the airless little world. Now Merlin's bones bleached on the plain, but the tape had come home and boot-legged copies commanded a high price in hidden markets. His camera's sharp eye had seen much.

There was the gate; there was the guardian. Gleaming, ageless, splendid. The robot stood 10 feet high, a square, blocky, black shape topped by the tiny anthropomorphic head dome, featureless and sleek. Behind him the gate, wide open but impassable all the same. And behind him, the treasure, culled from the craftsmanship of a thousand worlds, left here who knew why, untold years ago.

No mere jewels. No dreary slabs of so-called precious metal. The wealth here was not intrinsic; no vandal would think of melting the treasure into dead ingots. Here were statuettes of spun iron that seemed to move and breathe. Plaques of purest lead, engraved with lathework that dazzled the mind and made the heart hesitate. Cunning intaglios in granite, from the workshops of a frosty world half a parsec from nowhere. A scatter of opals, burning with an inner light, fashioned into artful loops of brightness.

A helix of rainbow-coloured wood. A series of interlocking strips of some beast's bone, bent and splayed so that the pattern blurred and perhaps abutted some other-dimensional continuum. Cleverly carved shells, one within the other, descending to infinity. Burnished leaves of nameless trees. Polished pebbles from unknown beaches. A dizzying spew of wonders, covering some 50 square yards, sprawled out behind the gate in stunning profusion.

Rough men unschooled in the tenets of aesthetics had given their lives to possess the treasure. It took no fancy knowledge to realise the wealth of it, to know that collectors strung from Galaxy to Galaxy would fight with bared fangs to claim their share. Gold bars did not a treasure make. But these things? Beyond duplication, almost beyond price?

Bolzano was wet with a fever of yearning before the tape had run its course. When it was over, he slumped in his chair, drained, depleted.

Dawn came. The silvery moons fell from the sky. The red sun splashed across the heavens. Bolzano allowed himself the luxury of an hour's sleep.

And then it was time to begin . . .

* * *

As a precautionary measure, they left the ship in a parking orbit three miles above the airless world. Past reports were unreliable, and there was no telling how far the robot guardian's power extended. If Lipescu were successful, Bolzano could descend and get him – and the treasure. If Lipescu failed, Bolzano would land and make his own attempt.

The big man looked even bigger, encased in his suit and in the outer casement of a dropshaft. Against his massive chest he wore the computer, an extra brain as lovingly crafted as any object in the treasure hoard. The guardian would ask him questions; the computer would help him answer. And Bolzano would listen. If Lipescu erred, possibly his partner could benefit by knowledge of the error and succeed.

"Can you hear me?" Lipescu asked.

"Perfectly. Go on, get going!"

"What's the hurry? Eager to see me die?"

"Are you that lacking in confidence?" Bolzano asked. "Do you want me to go first?"

"Fool," Lipescu muttered. "listen carefully. If I die, I don't want it to be in vain."

"What would it matter to you?"

The bulky figure wheeled around. Bolzano could not see his partner's face, but he knew Lipescu must be scowling. The giant rumbled, "Is life that valuable? Can't I take a risk?"

"For *my* benefit?"

"For mine," Lipescu said. "I'll be coming back."

"Go then. The robot is waiting."

Lipescu walked to the lock. A moment later he was through and gliding downward, a one-man spaceship, jets flaring beneath his feet. Bolzano settled by the scanner to watch. A televector pick-up homed in on Lipescu just as he made his landing, coming down in a blaze of fire. The treasure and its guardian lay about a mile away. Lipescu rid himself of the dropshaft, stepping with giant bounds towards the waiting guardian.

Bolzano watched.

Bolzano listened.

The televector pick-up provided full fidelity. It was useful for Bolzano's purposes, and useful, too, for Lipescu's vanity, for the big man wanted his every moment taped for posterity. It was interesting to see Lipescu dwarfed by the guardian. The black faceless robot, squat and motionless, topped the big man by more than three feet.

Lipescu said, "Step aside."

The robot's reply came in surprisingly human tones, though void of any distinquishing accent. "What I guard is not to be plundered."

"I claim them by right," Lipescu said.

"So have many others. But their right did not exist. Nor does yours. I cannot step aside for you."

"Test me," Lipescu said. "See if I have the right or not!"

"Only my master may pass."

"Who is your master? *I* am your master!"

"My master is he who can command me. And no one can command me who shows ignorance before me."

"Test me, then," Lipescu demanded.

"Death is the penalty for failure."

"Test me."

"The treasure does not belong to you."

"Test me and step aside."

"Your bones will join the rest here."

"Test me," Lipescu said.

Watching from aloft, Bolzano went tense. His thin body drew together like that of a chilled spider. Anything might happen now. The robot might propound riddles, like the Sphinx confronting Oedipus.

It might demand the proofs of mathematical theorems. It might ask the translation of strange words. So they gathered, from their knowledge of what had befallen other men here. And, so it seemed, to give a wrong answer was to earn instant death.

He and Lipescu had ransacked the libraries of the world. They had packed all knowledge, so they hoped, into their computer. It had taken months, even with multi-stage programming. The tiny shining glove of metal on Lipescu's chest contained an infinity of answers to an infinity of questions.

Below, there was long silence as man and robot studied one another. The guardian said, "Define latitude."

"Do you mean geographical latitude?" Lipescu asked.

Bolzano congealed with fear. The idiot, asking for a clarification! He would die before he began!

The robot said, "Define latitude."

Lipescu's voice was calm. "The angular distance of a point on a planet's surface north or south of the equator, as measured from the centre of the planet."

"Which is more consonant," the robot asked, "the minor third or the major sixth?"

There was a pause. Lipescu was no musician. But the computer would feed him the answer.

"The minor third," Lipescu said.

Without a pause, the robot fired another question. "Name the prime numbers between 5,237 and 7,641."

Bolzano smiled as Lipescu handled the question with ease. So far, so good. The robot had stuck to strictly factual questions, schoolbook stuff, posing no real problems to Lipescu. And after the initial hesitation and quibble over latitude, Lipescu had seemed to grow in confidence from moment to moment. Bolzano squinted at the scanner, looking beyond the robot, through the open gate, to the helter-skelter pile of treasures. He wondered which would fall to his lot when he and Lipescu divided them, two-thirds for Lipescu, the rest for him.

"Name the seven tragic poets of Elifora," the robot said.

"Domiphar, Halionis, Slegg, Hork-Sekan . . ."

"The 14 signs of the zodiac as seen from Morneez," the robot demanded.

"The Teeth, the Serpents, the Leaves, the Waterfall, the Blot . . ."

"What is a pedicel?"

"The stalk of an individual flower of an inflorescence."

"How many years did the Siege of Larrina last?"

"Eight."

"What did the flower cry in the third canto of Somner's *Vehicles*?"

" 'I ache, I sob, I whimper, I die,' " Lipescu boomed.

"Distinguish between the stamen and the pistil."

"The stamen is the pollen-producing organ of the flower; the pistil . . .

And so it went. Question after question. The robot was not content with the legendary three questions of mythology; it asked a dozen and then asked more. Lipescu answered perfectly, prompted by the murmuring of the peerless compendium of knowledge strapped to his chest. Bolzano kept careful count: the big man had dealt magnificently with 17 questions. When would the robot concede defeat? When would it end its grim quiz and step aside?

It asked an 18th question, pathetically easy. All it wanted was an exposition of the Pythagorean Theorem. Lipescu did not even need the computer for that. He answered, briefly, concisely, correctly. Bolzano was proud of his burly partner.

Then the robot struck Lipescu dead.

It happened in the flickering of an eyelid. Lipescu's voice had ceased, and he stood there, ready for the next question, but the next question did not come. Rather, a panel in the robot's vaulted belly slid open, and something bright and sinous lashed out, uncoiling over the 10 feet or so that separated guardian from challenger, and sliced Lipescu in half. The bright something slid back out of sight. Lipescu's trunk toppled to one side. His massive legs remained absurdly planted for a moment; then they crumpled, and a spacesuited leg kicked once, and all was still.

Stunned, Bolzano trembled in the loneliness of the cabin, and his lymph turned to water. What had gone wrong? Lipescu had given the proper answer to every question, and yet the robot had slain him. Why? Could the big man possibly have misphrased Pythagoras? No: Bolzano had listened. The answer had been flawless, as had the 17 that preceded it. Seemingly the robot had lost patience with the game, then. The robot had cheated.

Arbitrarily, maliciously, it had lashed out at Lipescu, punishing him for the correct answer.

Did robots cheat, Bolzano wondered? Could they act in malicious spite? No robot he knew was capable of such actions; but this robot was unlike all others.

For a long while, Bolzano remained huddled in the cabin. The temptation was strong to blast free of orbit and head home, treasureless but alive. Yet the treasure called to him. Some suicidal impulse drove him on. Siren-like, the robot drew him downward.

There had to be a way to make the robot yield, Bolzano thought, as he guided his small ship down the broad barren plain. Using the computer had been a good idea, whose only defect was that it hadn't worked. The records were uncertain, but it appeared that in the past men had died when they finally gave a wrong answer after a series of right ones. Lipescu had given no wrong answers. Yet he, too, had died. It was inconceivable that the robot understood some relationship of the squares on the hypotenuse and on the other two sides that was different from the relationship Lipescu had expressed.

Bolzano wondered what method would work.

He plodded leadenly across the plain towards the gate and its guardian. The germ of an idea formed on him as he walked doggedly on.

He was, he knew, condemned to death by his own greed. Only extreme agility of mind would save him from sharing Lipescu's fate. Ordinary intelligence would not work. Odyssean cleverness was the only salvation. Bolzano approached the robot. Bones lay everywhere. Lipescu weltered in his own blood. Against that vast dead chest lay the computer, Bolzano knew. But he shrank from reaching for it. He would do without it. He looked away, unwilling to let the sight of Lipescu's severed body interfere with the coolness of his thoughts.

He collected his courage. The robot showed no interest in him.

"Give ground," Bolzano said. "I am here. I come for the treasure."

"Win your right to it."

"What must I do?"

"Demonstrate truth," the robot said. "Reveal inwardness. Display understanding."

"I am ready," said Bolzano.

The robot offered a question. "What is the excretory unit of the vertebrate kidney called?"

Bolzano contemplated. He had no idea. The computer could tell him, but the computer lay strapped to fallen Lipescu. No matter. The robot wanted truth, inwardness, understanding. Lipescu had offered information. Lipescu had perished.

"The frog in the pond," Bolzano said, "utters an azure cry."

There was silence. Bolzano watched the robot's front, waiting for the panel to slide open, the sinuous something to chop him in half.

The robot said, "During the War of Dogs on Vanderveer IX, the embattled colonists drew up 38 dogmas of defiance. Quote the third, the ninth, the twenty-second, and the thirty-fifth."

Bolzano pondered. This was an alien robot, product of an unknown hand. How did its maker's mind work? Did it respect knowledge? Did it treasure facts for their own sake? Or did it recognise that information is meaningless, insight a nonlogical process?

Lipescu had been logical. He lay in pieces.

"The mereness of pain," Bolzano responded, "is ineffable and refreshing."

The robot said, "The monastery of Kwaisen was besieged by the soldiers of Oda Nobunaga on April 3, 1582. What words of wisdom did the abbot utter?"

Bolzano spoke quickly and buoyantly. "Eleven, forty-one, elephant, voluminous."

The last word slipped from his lips despite an effort to retrieve it.

Elephants *were* voluminous, he thought. A fatal slip? The robot did not appear to notice. Sonorously, ponderously the great machine delivered the next question.

"What is the percentage of oxygen in the atmosphere of the planet Muldonar VII?"

"False witness bears a swift sword," Bolzano replied.

The robot made an odd humming sound. Abruptly it rolled on massive treads, moving some six feet to its left. The gate of the treasure trove stood wide, beckoning.

"You may enter," the robot said.

Bolzano's heart leaped. He had won! He had gained the high prize!

Others had failed, most recently less than an hour before, and their bones glistened on the plain. They had tried to answer the robot, sometimes giving right answers, sometimes giving wrong ones, and they had died. Bolzano lived.

It was a miracle, he thought. Luck? Shrewdness? Some of each, he told himself. He had watched a man give 18 right answers and die. So the accuracy of the responses did not matter to the robot. What did? Inwardness. Understanding. Truth.

There could be inwardness and understanding and truth in random answers, Bolzano realised. Where earnest striving had failed, mockery had succeeded. He had staked his life on nonsense, and the prize was his.

He staggered forward, into the treasure trove. Even in the light gravity, his feet were like leaden weights. Tension ebbed in him. He knelt among the treasures.

The tapes, the sharp-eyed televector scanners, had not begun to indicate the splendour of what lay here. Bolzano stared in awe and rapture at a tiny disk, no greater in diameter than a man's eye, on which myriad coiling lines writhed and twisted in patterns of rare beauty. He caught his breath, sobbing with the pain of perception as a gleaming marble spire, angled in mysterious swerves, came into view. Here, a bright beetle of some fragile waxy substance rested on a pedestal of yellow jade. There, a tangle of metallic cloth spurted dizzying patterns of luminescence. And over there – and beyond – and there . . .

The ransom of a universe, Bolzano thought.

It would take many trips to carry all this to his ship. Perhaps it would be better to bring the ship to the hoard, eh? He wondered, though, if he would lose his advantage if he stepped back through the gate. Was it possible that he would have to win entrance all over again? And would the robot accept his answers as willingly the second time?

It was something he would have to chance, Bolzano decided. His nimble mind worked out a plan. He would select a dozen, two dozen of the finest treasures, as much as he could comfortably carry, and take them back to the ship. Then he would lift the ship and set it down next to the gate. If the robot raised objections about his entering, Bolzano would simply depart, taking what he had already secured. There was no point in running undue risks. When he had sold this cargo, and felt pinched for money, he could always return and try to win admission once again. Certainly, no one else would steal the horde if he abandoned it.

Selection, that was the key now.

Crouching, Bolzano picked through the treasure, choosing for portability and easy marketability. The marble spire? Too big. But the coiling disk, yes, certainly, and the beetle, of course, and this small statuette of dull hue, and the cameos showing scenes no human eye had ever beheld, and this, and this, and this . . .

His pulse raced. His heart thundered. He saw himself travelling from world to world, vending his wares. Collectors, museums, governments would vie with one another to have these prizes. He would let them bid each object up into the millions before he sold. And, of course, he would keep one or two for himself – or perhaps three or four – souvenirs of this great adventure.

And someday when wealth bored him he would return and face the challenge again. And he would dare the robot to question him, and he would reply with random absurdities, demonstrating his grasp on the fundamental insight that in knowledge there is only hollow merit, and the robot would admit him once more to the treasure trove.

Bolzano rose. He cradled his lovelies in his arms. Carefully, carefully, he thought. Turning, he made his way through the gate.

The robot had not moved. It had shown no interest as Bolzano plundered the hoard. The small man walked calmly past it.

The robot said, "Why have you taken those? What do you want with them?"

Bolzano smiled. Nonchalantly he replied, "I've taken them because they're beautiful. Because I want them. Is there a better reason?"

"No," the robot said, and the panel slid open in its ponderous black chest.

Too late, Bolzano realised that the test had not yet ended, that the robot's question had arisen out of no idle curiosity. And this time he had replied in earnest, speaking in rational terms.

Bolzano shrieked. He saw the brightness coming towards him.

Death followed instantly.

The day Volman died

BY PHILIP DUNN

AS USUAL, at exactly 6.00 am in the morning, Sergeant Volman's fat, bloated face appeared on the wall-screens of Hut Nine and began screaming orders at the 25 men who lived and worked in the small mining establishment of Kasbol, located deep in the remote hill regions of Askangol.

"You scum are not pulling your weight," the voice from the screen raged. "We expect 20 barrels of Protaginash a week here, and H.Q. will be furious because these quotas are falling disgracefully short." Volman's face twisted into an ugly scowl and his voice became laced with venom. "In future, you will keep mining until the correct daily quantities are produced, regardless of the hours that you take to do this."

Volman then detailed the day's routine, allocating certain men to specific duties, gruffly shouting orders and instructions.

Despite their intense hatred for the arrogant task-master, the men leapt to work, sick with rage at the extra hours the new instructions entailed. No one in the grim and awful establishment dared even to think of defying the unseen tyrant. His power and authority were absolute.

Zevi Hagarin was a middle-aged, bulky miner who had spent his entire working life in Kasbol mine, ever since that terrible day 25 years ago when the tyrranical Proll party had seized power.

"How I hate and detest this stinking hole," the big man groaned bitterly, as he toiled alongside a companion deep beneath the surface, despair and frustration crept into his voice. "I'd do anything to get out of here – anything! I would die happily if only I could strangle that swine Volman to death very, very slowly."

Hagarin's workmate was a younger man in his late 20's. Petran Zacc swung his pick into the face of the narrow and gloomily-lit tunnel and then stooped to pick out the small pieces of Protaginash resulting from the miniature fall.

"Just forget about it, Hagarin," he said. "There isn't a thing we can do. We are totally and absolutely helpless. Just obey orders and try not to think of all the injustices we suffer. It's the same everywhere in Askangol these days. What's the point in brooding on it?" He shook his head wisely. "We have to make the best of a bad job."

"We're no better than filthy prisoners in a *concentration camp*," Hagarin moaned, ignoring the other man's advice. Sweat poured all over him, generated by a burning rage within him, as he smashed his pick violently into the never-ending face of the tunnel. "I've been here 25 years and they are never going to give me a break and find me work elsewhere. I know that now. Swines! Rats! I'd like that cursed wall of rock to be Volman's ugly face right now!"

At the end of a longer-than-usual day, the barrels of Protaginash were rolled out into the centre of the mining camp. The huge helicopter which flew in once a week arrived, dropping down from the surrounding hills, and the miners toiled to load the barrels. The crew of the helicopter watched indifferently from their cabin, aloof and uncommunicative. As soon as the operation was complete, the heavily-laden machine lumbered off into the sky again.

"How I'd love to be on that thing," a long-term miner agonised as the men watched the helicopter disappearing behind the hills. "Anything to get out of this hole."

"Don't even think of it," advised Zacc. "If the crew didn't spot you, Volman would. You can bet the swine has his piggy eyes fixed on us all the time."

They turned to stare at the only brick-built building within the camp. Set close to the perimeter of the mine, it was the one place where all personnel were absolutely forbidden to go. Without doubt, that was where Volman lived, watching everyone on his two-way screens and yelling orders through loudspeakers. They could almost feel the tyrant's eyes boring into them from the single small window set into one side of the building.

Suddenly Volman's voice bellowed out at them through the loudspeaker system. "Don't stand there like a pack of dummies! Back to your hut, scum!"

* * *

The following morning a terrible shock awaited the men of mining establishment Kasbol. Volman's face failed, for the first time ever, to appear on the hut screens.

The miners were in a state of shock and confusion. Without the Sergeant's detailed orders, it was quite impossible to commence work. No one other than Volman was permitted to assign duties.

"What could have happened?" groaned one of the men. "Why doesn't Volman appear on the screens. It's unnerving!"

The hours passed.

Zevi Hagarin rose from his bunk and stared at the nearest blank screen. "Something's happened to him," he declared, starting to pace up and down the hut in agitated, nervous excitement. "Volman's had an accident or he's been taken ill. He's dead! It's the *only* possible explanation!"

The other men reacted to his statement with incredulous gasps.

"Here's our chance to get of here," Hagarin called out, a note of almost hysterical elation registering in his voice. "He's dead and he can't activate the electric fence if we try to leave. We can walk out of here and lose ourselves in the forests behind the hills. The skunks will never find us!"

"No! Don't be a fool!" another of the miners shouted. "Suppose he is

just testing us? It's a trick! He wants to see what our reaction is. We'll be in terrible trouble if he is sitting there watching us all the time."

The men were fearful and uncertain. Every one of them longed for the freedom of the forests, yet the terrible fear of Sergeant Volman meant that none dare risk leaving unless it was certain that he was dead.

Petran Zacc suddenly shot off his own bunk and strode swiftly over to the nearest screen. Everyone watched him, surprised and tense.

"What are you going to do. Petran?"

"Find out if Volman really is there," Zacc answered, turning to grin at the staring, open-mouthed miners. He looked back at the screen. "Volman! You are a nasty, fat, stinking rat! We hate your guts. All of us! You are the vilest thing ever to crawl out of a sewer!" He shouted the insults, voice burning with intense hatred.

There was a loud gasp, followed by moans of horror and dread. Everyone expected to see Volman's face flash on to the screen, purple with fury, screaming threats and punishments at the miners. Even Petran Zacc was tensed with fear, dreading the ghastly prospect.

But nothing happened.

Zacc relaxed with a hissing sigh of relief. "If Volman really was there, he wouldn't tolerate such insults," he told his companions. "I gambled he was dead. Remember we had orders to increase our outputs? Well if that vile pig was merely testing us, he would be responsible for a greater loss of output, wouldn't he? We've wasted four hours already!"

The miners whooped and went wild. For the first time ever, there were scenes of immense joy and happiness in Hut Nine.

Everybody rushed to gather essential items of clothing and equipment and supplies of food.

"We'll establish our *own* community deep in the forest," Hagarin told the others gleefully. "It will be rough at first, but after a while we'll learn all the tricks of survival. We're free, comrades! Free of the tyrants! Free of this ghastly dump! Free to run our own lives! Let's go! Let's get out of here!"

Within two hours the freedom-seekers were ready to leave. Yelling and whooping, the miners rushed towards the only gateway built in the massive perimeter fence. Normally electrified at night, or in the unlikely event that a worker tried to leave the place in daytime, a single hefty kick from Zevi Hagarin smashed the gate away from the lock that fastened it.

Hagarin suddenly held up both hands and roared for silence.

"Wait! Before we go, let's take a look inside Volman's quarters. I want to set my eyes on that rat at last and see him lying in there dead."

A roar of approval greeted this remark.

Only Zacc cried out in dissent. "No!" he protested loudly. Forget Volman and everything else about this rotten place. Let's just get out of here while we still have the chance." The young miner's voice rose in anguish and pleading. "We are only one step from freedom, comrades. Don't let's risk losing everything now!"

But everyone else wanted to look in the one place that they were all normally forbidden even to approach. Zacc was overruled by the majority. So, now subdued and nervous, eyes wide with eager anticipation, the freedom-seekers stalked over to the low, flat-roofed, brick building. There was a door at the rear, a few metres from the perimeter fence.

"Open it then!" someone whispered nervously at Hagarin. "Let's take a look inside!"

The swarthy middle-aged miner fought back the terror that even now threatened to prevent him performing the simple task. The ingrained fear of Volman was difficult to rid himself of, despite the present circumstances. Then, taking a grip of himself at last, Hagarin grasped the handle and flung the door open.

A stunned gasp of shock and disbelief filled the air. The interior of the building was but one single large room, filled on all sides with complex, elaborate panels and electronic apparatus. Trembling, bewildered, the miners entered slowly and stared uncomprehendingly at the lifeless bulk of inactive machinery.

"Where is Volman? What is all this stuff for?" someone whispered.

Hagarin noticed a small silver object lying on the floor. It was identical to a dozen others set into a panel directly in front of him. The miner picked the component up and stared at it stupidly, wonderingly. There was an empty space in the panel and, suddenly curious, Hagarin reached across to see if the thing fitted into the gap.

Zacc turned and saw what he was doing. A flash of understanding and horror twisted across his features. "Don't put that back, Hagarin!" he screamed. "In the name of mercy, leave it alone!"

But it was too late. Instantly, the whole of the apparatus began to hum and lights began to flash. The startled trespassers shrieked with horror as Volman's face appeared on a screen set within the room. The image distorted wildly with hate and rage.

"Scum! Trash! Get out of here! Back to your work, pigs! You'll all work extra shifts! Half rations for the rest of the week! Move! Get out!"

Mad with terror, the miners fled from the control room, back towards the work areas.

Only Zacc understood. Desperately he screamed at his companions.

"In the name of mercy, don't you understand? Volman does not exist! This place is run by a computer. Volman isn't real. He can't hurt you! We have been terrorised by a monstrous bluff. We can still get out of here!" But his agonised shrieks fell on deaf ears.

Volman's fat face appeared on one of the outside screens. His voice screamed orders at the mob of panic-stricken, yelling miners.

"Zacc is a filthy traitor! Arrest him! Take him to the punishment block and flog him. You, Hagarin, shall wield the whip. Move! Move!"

Within seconds, Petran Zacc found himself seized and dragged away by his companions. His screams and pleas were utterly wasted. And then with sickening horror he understood that the dream of freedom was ended.

This time for ever.

Computers don't argue

BY GORDON R. DICKSON

Treasure Book Club

PLEASE DO NOT FOLD,
SPINDLE OR MUTILATE
THIS CARD

Mr.: Walter A. Child Balance $4.98 Dear Customer: Enclosed is your latest book selection. "Kidnapped", by Robert Louis Stevenson.

437 Woodlawn Drive
Panduk, Michigan
Nov. 16, 1965

Treasure Book Club
1823 Mandy Street
Chicago, Illinois

Dear Sirs:

I wrote you recently about the computer punch card you sent, billing me for "Kim", by Rudyard Kipling. I did not open the package containing it until I had already posted my cheque for the amount on the card. On opening the package, I found the book missing half its pages. I sent it back to you, requesting either another copy or my money back. Instead, you have sent me a copy of "Kidnapped", by Robert Louis Stevenson. Will you please straighten this out?

I hereby return the copy of "Kidnapped".

Sincerely yours,
Walter A. Child

Treasure Book Club

SECOND NOTICE
PLEASE DO NOT FOLD,
SPINDLE OR MUTILATE
THIS CARD

Mr.: Walter A. Child Balance: $4.98 for "Kidnapped", by Robert Louis Stevenson.
(If remittance has been made for the above, please disregard this notice.)

437 Woodlawn Drive
Panduk, Michigan
Jan. 21, 1966

Treasure Book Club
1823 Mandy Street
Chicago, Illinois

Dear Sirs:

May I direct your attention to my letter of November 16, 1965? You are still continuing to dun me with computer punch cards for a book I did not order. Whereas, actually, it is your company that owes *me* money.

Sincerely yours,
Walter A. Child

TREASURE BOOK CLUB
1823 Mandy Street
Chicago, Illinois
Feb. 1, 1966

Mr. Walter A. Child
437 Woodlawn Drive
Panduk, Michigan

Dear Mr. Child:

We have sent you a number of reminders concerning an amount owing to us as a result of book purchases you have made from us. This amount, which is $4.98, is now long overdue.

This situation is disappointing to us, particularly since there was no hesitation on our part in extending you credit at the time original arrangements for these purchases were made by you. If we do not receive payment in full by return post, we will be forced to turn the matter over to a collection agency.

Very truly yours,
Samuel P. Grimes
Collection Mgr.

---

437 Woodlawn Drive
Panduk, Michigan
Feb. 5, 1966

Mr. Samuel P. Grimes
Treasure Book Club
1823 Mandy Street
Chicago, Illinois

Dear Mr. Grimes:

Will you stop sending me punch cards and form letters and make me some kind of a direct answer from a human being?

I don't owe you money. *You* owe me money. Maybe I should turn your company over to a collection agency.

Walter A. Child

Mr. Walter A. Child
437 Woodlawn Drive
Panduk, Michigan

FEDERAL COLLECTION OUTFIT
88 Prince Street, Chicago, Illinois
Feb. 28, 1966

Dear Mr. Child:

Your account with the Treasure Book Club, of $4.98 plus interest and charges, has been turned over to our agency for collection. The amount due is now $6.83. Please send your cheque for this amount or we shall be forced to take immediate action.

Jacob N. Harshe
Vice-President

Mr. Walter A. Child
437 Woodlawn Drive
Panduk, Michigan

FEDERAL COLLECTION OUTFIT
88 Prince Street, Chicago, Illinois
April 8, 1966

Dear Mr. Child:

You have seen fit to ignore our courteous requests to settle your long overdue account with the Treasure Book Club, which is now, with accumulated interest and charges, in the amount of $7.51.

If payment in full is not forthcoming by April 11, 1966 we will be forced to turn the matter over to our attorneys for immediate court action.

Ezekiel B. Harshe
President

MALONEY, MAHONEY,
MACNAMARA AND PRUITT
Attorneys

Mr. Walter A. Child
437 Woodlawn Drive
Panduk, Michigan

89 Prince Street
Chicago, Illinois
April 29, 1966

Dear Mr. Child:

Your indebtedness to the Treasure Book Club has been referred to us for legal action to collect.

This indebtedness is now in the amount of $10.01. If you will send us this amount so that we may receive it before May 5, 1966, the matter may be satisfied. However, if we do not receive satisfaction in full by that date, we will take steps to collect through the courts.

I am sure you will see the advantage of avoiding a judgment against you, which as a matter of record would do lasting harm to your credit ratings.

Very truly yours,
Hagthorpe M. Pruitt, Jr.
Attorney at law

437 Woodlawn Drive
Panduk, Michigan
May 4, 1966

Mr. Hagthorpe M. Pruitt, Jr.
Maloney, Mahoney, MacNamara and Pruitt
89 Prince Street
Chicago, Illinois

Dear Mr. Pruitt:

You don't know what a pleasure it is to me in this matter to get a letter from a live human being to whom I can explain the situation.

This whole matter is silly. I explained it fully in my letters to the Treasure Book Company. But I might as well have been trying to explain to the computer that puts out their punch cards, for all the good it seemed to do. Briefly, what happened was I ordered a copy of "Kim", by Rudyard Kipling, for $4.98. When I opened the package they sent me, I found the book had only half its pages, but I'd previously posted a cheque to pay them for the book.

I sent the book back to them, asking either for a whole copy or my money back. Instead, they sent me a copy of "Kidnapped", by Robert Louis Stevenson – which I had not ordered; and for which they have been trying to collect from me.

Meanwhile, I am still waiting for the money back that they owe me for the copy of "Kim" that I didn't get. That's the whole story. Maybe you can help me straighten them out.

Relievedly yours,
Walter A. Child

P.S.: I also sent them back their copy of "Kidnapped", as soon as I got it, but it hasn't seemed to help. They have never even acknowledged getting it back.

MALONEY, MAHONEY,
MACNAMARA AND PRUITT
Attorneys

Mr. Walter A. Child
437 Woodlawn Drive
Panduk, Michigan

89 Prince Street
Chicago, Illinois
May 9, 1966

Dear Mr. Child:

I am in possession of no information indicating that any item purchased by you from the Treasure Book Club has been returned.

I would hardly think that, if the case had been as you stated, the Treasure Book Club would have retained us to collect the amount owing from you.

If I do not receive your payment in full within three days, by May 12, 1966, we will be forced to take legal action.

Very truly yours,
Hagthorpe M. Pruitt, Jr.

COURT OF MINOR CLAIMS
Chicago, Illinois

Mr. Walter A. Child
437 Woodlawn Drive
Panduk, Michigan

Be informed that a judgment was taken and entered against you in this court this day of May 26, 1966 in the amount of $15.66 including court costs.

Payment in satisfaction of this judgment may be made to this court or to the adjudged creditor. In the case of payment being made to the creditor, a release should be obtained from the creditor and filed with this court in order to free you of legal obligation in connection with this judgment.

Under the recent Reciprocal Claims Act, if you are a citizen of a different state, a duplicate claim may be automatically entered and judged against you in your own state so that collection may be made there as well as in the State of Illinois.

COURT OF MINOR CLAIMS
Chicago, Illinois

PLEASE DO NOT FOLD,
SPINDLE OR MUTILATE THIS CARD

Judgment was passed this day of May 27, 1966 under Statute $15.66
Against: Child, Walter A. of 437 Woodlawn Drive, Panduk, Michigan.
Pray to enter a duplicate claim for judgment
In: Picayune Court – Panduk, Michigan
For Amount: Statute 941

437 Woodlawn Drive
Panduk, Michigan
May 31, 1966

Samuel P. Grimes
Treasure Book Club
1823 Mandy Street
Chicago, Illinois

Grimes:

This business has gone far enough. I've got to come down to Chicago on business on my own tomorrow. I'll see you then and we'll get this straightened out once and for all, about who owes what to whom, and how much!

Yours,
Walter A. Child

From the desk of the Clerk
Picayune Court

June 1, 1966

Harry:

The attached computer card from Chicago's Minor Claims Court against A. Walter has a 1500-series Statute number on it. That puts it over in Criminal with you, rather than Civil, with me. So I herewith submit it for your computer instead of mine. How's business?

Joe

CRIMINAL RECORDS
Panduk, Michigan

PLEASE DO NOT FOLD,
SPINDLE OR MUTILATE THIS CARD

Convicted: (Child) A. Walter
On: May 26, 1966
Address: 437 Woodlawn Drive, Panduk, Mich.
Crim: Statute: 1566 (Corrected) 1567
Crime: Kidnap
Date: Nov. 16, 1965
Notes: At large. To be picked up at once.

POLICE DEPARTMENT, PANDUK, MICHIGAN. TO POLICE DEPARTMENT CHICAGO, ILLINOIS. CONVICTED SUBJECT A. (COMPLETE FIRST NAME UNKNOWN) WALTER, SOUGHT HERE IN CONNECTION REF. YOUR NOTIFICATION OF JUDGMENT FOR KIDNAP OF CHILD NAMED ROBERT LOUIS STEVENSON, ON NOV. 16, 1965. INFORMATION HERE INDICATES SUBJECT FLED HIS RESIDENCE, AT 437 WOODLAWN DRIVE, PANDUK, AND MAY BE AGAIN IN YOUR AREA.

POSSIBLE CONTACT IN YOUR AREA: THE TREASURE BOOK CLUB, 1823 MANDY STREET, CHICAGO, ILLINOIS. SUBJECT NOT KNOWN TO BE ARMED, BUT PRESUMED DANGEROUS. PICK UP AND HOLD, ADVISING US OF CAPTURE . . .

TO POLICE DEPARTMENT, PANDUK, MICHIGAN, REFERENCE YOUR REQUEST TO PICK UP AND HOLD A. (COMPLETE FIRST NAME UNKNOWN) WALTER, WANTED IN PANDUK ON STATUTE 1567, CRIME OF KIDNAPPING.

SUBJECT ARRESTED AT OFFICES OF TREASURE BOOK

CLUB, OPERATING THERE UNDER ALIAS WALTER ANTHONY CHILD AND ATTEMPTING TO COLLECT $4.98 FROM ONE SAMUEL P. GRIMES, EMPLOYEE OF THAT COMPANY. DISPOSAL: HOLDING FOR YOUR ADVICE.

POLICE DEPARTMENT PANDUK, MICHIGAN TO POLICE DEPARTMENT CHICAGO, ILLINOIS.

REF: A. WALTER (ALIAS WALTER ANTHONY CHILD) SUBJECT WANTED FOR CRIME OF KIDNAP, YOUR AREA, REF: YOUR COMPUTER PUNCH CARD NOTIFICATION OF JUDGMENT, DATED MAY 27, 1966. COPY OUR CRIMINAL RECORDS PUNCH CARD HEREWITH FORWARDED TO YOUR COMPUTER SECTION.

CRIMINAL RECORDS
Chicago, Illinois

PLEASE DO NOT FOLD,
SPINDLE OR MUTILATE THIS CARD

SUBJECT (CORRECTION – OMITTED RECORD SUPPLIED)
APPLICABLE STATUTE NO. 1567
JUDGMENT NO. 456789
TRIAL RECORD: APPARENTLY MISFILED AND UNAVAILABLE
DIRECTION: TO APPEAR FOR SENTENCING BEFORE JUDGE JOHN ALEXANDER MCDIVOT, COURTROOM A, JUNE 9, 1966

From the Desk of Judge Alexander J. McDivot

June 2, 1966

Dear Tony:

I've got an adjudged criminal coming up before me for sentencing on Thursday morning – but the trial transcript is apparently misfiled.

I need some kind of information (Ref: A. Walter – Judgment No. 456789, Criminal). For example, what about the victim of the kidnapping. Was the victim harmed?

Jack McDivot

June 3, 1966

Records Search Unit
Re: Ref: Judgement No. 456789 – victim is dead.

Tonio Malagasi
Records Division

To: United States Statistics Office June 3, 1966
Attn: Information Section
Subject: Robert Louis Stevenson
Query: Information concerning

Records Search Unit
Criminal Records Division
Police Department
Chicago, Ill.

To: Records Search Unit June 5, 1966
Criminal Records Division
Police Department
Chicago, Illinois
Subject: Your Query re Robert Louis Stevenson (File No. 189623)
Action: Subject deceased. Age at death, 44 yrs. Further information requested?

A.K.
Information Section
U.S. Statistics Office

To: United States Statistics Office June 6, 1966
Attn: Information Division
Subject: Re: File No. 189623
No further information required.

Thank you.
Records Search Unit
Criminal Records Division
Police Department
Chicago, Illinois.

To: Tonio Malagasi June 7, 1966
Records Division
Re: Ref: Judgment No. 456789 – victim is dead.

Records Search Unit

To: Judge Alexander J. McDivot's Chambers June 7, 1966
Dear Jack:
Ref: Judgment No. 456789. The victim in this kidnap case was apparently slain.

From the strange lack of background information on the killer and his victim, as well as the victim's age, this smells to me like a gangland killing. This for your information. Don't quote me. It seems to me, though, that Stevenson – the victim – has a name that rings a faint bell with me. Possibly, one of the East Coast Mob, since the association comes back to me as something about pirates – possibly New York dock hijackers – and something about buried loot.

As I say, above is only speculation for your private guidance.

Any time I can help . . .

Best,
Tony Malagasi
Records Division

MICHAEL R. REYNOLDS
Attorney-at-law

49 Water Street
Chicago, Illinois
June 8, 1966

Dear Tim:

Regrets: I can't make the fishing trip. I've been court-appointed here to represent a man about to be sentenced tomorrow on a kidnapping charge.

Ordinarily, I might have tried to beg off, and McDivot, who is doing the sentencing, would probably have turned me loose. But this is the damndest thing you ever heard of.

The man being sentenced has apparently been not only charged, but adjudged guilty as a result of a comedy of errors too long to go into here. He not only isn't guilty – he's got the best case I ever heard of for damages against one of the larger Book Clubs headquartered here in Chicago. And that's a case I wouldn't mind taking on.

It's inconceivable – but damnably possible. Once you stop to think of it in this day and age of machine-made records – that a completely innocent man could be put in this position.

There shouldn't be much to it. I've asked to see McDivot tomorrow before the time of sentencing, and it'll just be a matter of explaining to him. Then I can discuss the damage suit with my freed client at his leisure.

Fishing next weekend?

Yours,
Mike

MICHAEL R. REYNOLDS
Attorney-at-law

49 Water Street
Chicago, Illinois
June 10

Dear Tim:

In haste . . .

No fishing this coming week either. Sorry.

You won't believe it. My innocent-as-a-lamb-and-I'm-not-kidding client has just been sentenced to death for first-degree murder in connection with the death of his kidnap victim.

Yes, I explained the whole thing to McDivot. And when he explained his situation to me, I nearly fell out of my chair.

It wasn't a matter of my not convincing him. It took less than three minutes to show him that my client should never have been within the walls of the Court Jail for a second. But – get this – McDivot couldn't do a thing about it.

The point is, my man had already been judged guilty according to the computerised records. In the absence of a trial record – of course there never was one (but that's something I'm not free to explain to you now) – the judge has to go by what records are available. And in the case of an adjudged prisoner, McDivot's only legal choice was whether to sentence to life imprisonment, or execution.

The death of the kidnap victim, according to the statute, made the death penalty mandatory. Under the new law governing length of time for appeal, which has been shortened because of the new system of computerising records, to force an elimination of unfair delay and mental anguish to those condemned. I have five days in which to file an appeal, and ten to have it acted on.

Needless to say, I am not going to monkey with an appeal. I'm going directly to the Governor for a pardon – after which we will get this farce reversed. McDivot has already written the Governor, also, explaining that his sentence was ridiculous, but that he had no choice. Between the two of us, we ought to have a pardon in short order.

Then, I'll make the fur fly . . .

And we'll get in some fishing.

Best,
Mike

OFFICE OF THE GOVERNOR OF ILLINOIS

Mr. Michael R. Reynolds June 17, 1966
49 Water Street
Chicago, Illinois

Dear Mr. Reynolds:

In reply to your query about the request for pardon for Walter A. Child (A. Walter), may I inform you that the Governor is still on his trip with the Midwest Governors Committee, examining the Wall in Berlin. He should be back next Friday.

I will bring your request and letters to his attention the minute he returns.

Very truly yours,
Clara B. Jilks
Secretary to the Governor

Michael R. Reynolds June 27, 1966
49 Water Street
Chicago, Illinois

Dear Mike:

Where is that pardon?

My execution date is only five days from now!

Walt

Walter A. Child (A. Walter) June 29, 1966
Cell Block E
Illinois State Penitentiary
Joliet, Illinois

Dear Walt:

The Governor returned, but was called away immediately to the White House in Washington to give his views on interstate sewage.

I am camping on his doorstep and will be on him the moment he arrives here.

Meanwhile, I agree with you about the seriousness of the situation. The warden at the prison there, Mr. Allen Magruder, will bring this letter to you and have a private talk with you. I urge you to listen to what he has to say; and I enclose letters from your family also urging you to listen to Warden Magruder.

Yours,
Mike

Michael R. Reynolds June 30, 1966
49 Water Street
Chicago, Illinois

Dear Mike: (This letter being smuggled out by Warden Magruder)

As I was talking to Warden Magruder in my cell, here, news was brought to him that the Governor has at last returned for a while to Illinois, and will be in his office early tomorrow morning, Friday. So you will have time to get the pardon signed by him and delivered to the prison in time to stop my execution on Saturday.

Accordingly, I have turned down the Warden's kind offer of a chance to escape; since he told me he could by no means guarantee to have all the guards out of my way when I tried it; and there was a chance of my being killed escaping.

But now everything will straighten itself out. Actually, an experience as fantastic as this had to break down sometime under its own weight.

Best,
Walt

FOR THE SOVEREIGN STATE OF ILLINOIS

I, Hubert Daniel Willikens, Governor of the State of Illinois, and invested with the authority and powers appertaining thereto, including the power to pardon those in my judgment wrongfully convicted or otherwise deserving of executive mercy, do this day of July 1, 1966 announce and proclaim that Walter A. Child (A. Walter) now in custody as a consequence of erroneous conviction upon a crime of which he is entirely innocent, is fully and freely pardoned of said crime. And I do direct the necessary authorities having custody of the said Walter A. Child (A. Walter) in whatever place or places he may be held, to immediately free, release, and allow unhindered departure to him . . .

Interdepartmental Routing Service

PLEASE DO NOT FOLD, MUTILATE,
OR SPINDLE THIS CARD

Failure to route Document properly.
To: Governor Hubert Daniel Willikens
Re: Pardon issued to Walter A. Child, July 1, 1966
Dear State Employee:

You have failed to attach your Routing Number.

PLEASE: Resubmit document with this card and form 876, explaining your authority for placing a TOP RUSH category on this document. Form 876 must be signed by your Departmental Superior.

RESUBMIT ON: Earliest possible date ROUTING SERVICE office is open. In this case, Tuesday, July 5, 1966.

WARNING: Failure to submit form 876 WITH THE SIGNATURE OF YOUR SUPERIOR may make you liable to prosecution for misusing a Service of the State Government. A warrant may be issued for your arrest.

There are NO exceptions. YOU have been WARNED.

Great Lost Discoveries — II

Invulnerability

BY FREDRIC BROWN

THE SECOND GREAT LOST DISCOVERY was the secret of invulnerability. It was discovered in 1952 by a United States Navy radar officer, Lieutenant Paul Hickendorf. The device was electronic and consisted of a small box that could be carried handily in a pocket; when a switch on the box was turned on the person carrying the device was surrounded by a force field whose strength, as far as it could be measured by Hickendorf's excellent mathematics, was as near as matters to infinite.

The field was also completely impervious to any degree of heat and any quantity of radiation.

Lieutenant Hickendorf decided that a man – or a woman or a child or a dog – enclosed in that force field could withstand the explosion of a hydrogen bomb at close range and not be injured in the slightest degree.

No hydrogen bomb had been exploded up to that time, but at the moment he completed his device, the lieutenant happened to be on a ship, cruiser class, that was steaming across the Pacific Ocean en route to an atoll called Eniwetok, and the fact had leaked out that they were to be there to assist in the first explosion of a hydrogen bomb.

Lieutenant Hickendorf decided to get lost – to hide out on the target island and be there when the bomb went off, thereby demonstrating beyond all doubt that his discovery was workable, a defence against the most powerful weapon of all time.

It proved difficult but he concealed himself successfully and was there, only yards away from the H-bomb – after having crept closer and closer during the countdown – when it exploded.

His calculations had been completely correct and he was not injured in the slightest way, not scratched, not bruised, not burned.

But Lieutenant Hickendorf had overlooked the possibility of one thing happening, and that one thing happened. He was blown off the surface of the earth with much more than escape velocity.

Straight out, not even into orbit. Forty-nine days later he fell into the sun, still completely uninjured but unfortunately long since dead since the force field had carried with it enough air to last him only a few hours, and so his discovery was lost to mankind, at least for the duration of the 20th-century.

An honest day's work

BY HARRY HARRISON

"I DO MY JOB, that's all. And that's all that anyone can expect." Jerry's jaw set hard with these words, set as firmly as his voice as he bit deep into the scarred stem of the old pipe.

"I know that, Mr. Cruncher," the Lieutenant said. "No one is asking you to do anything more than that, or to do anything wrong." He was dusty and one of the pocket flaps had been torn off his uniform. There was a wild look in his eye and he had a tendency to talk too fast. "We tracked you down through BuRecCent and it wasn't easy, there were good men lost . . ." His voice started to rise and he drew himself up with an effort. "We would like your co-operation if we could get it."

"Not the sort of thing I like to do. It could lead to trouble."

* * *

The trouble was that no one expected it, or rather the people who expected it had expected something altogether different and had made their plans accordingly and fed them to the computer which had drawn up programs covering all possible variations of the original. However the Betelgeuseans had a completely different plan in mind so they therefore succeeded far beyond what was possibly their own wildest dreams. The trade station they had set up in Tycho crater on the Moon was just that, a trade station, and had nothing to do at all with the events that followed.

Records of the Disaster are confused, as well they might be under the circumstances, and the number of aliens involved in the first phase of the invasion was certainly only a fraction of the exaggerated figures that were being tossed around by excited newsmen, or worried military personnel who felt that there *must* be that number of attacking aliens to wreak the damage that was done. The chances are that there were no more than two, three maximum, ships involved; a few hundred Betelgeuseans at the most. A few hundred to subjugate an entire planet – and they came within a hair of succeeding.

* * *

"Colonel, this is Mr. Cruncher who has volunteered . . ."

"A *civilian*! Will you get him the hell out of here and blindfold him first, you unutterable fool. This headquarters is double-red-zed top security . . .!"

"Sir, the security doesn't matter any more. All of our communications are shut down, we're sealed off from the troops."

"Quiet, you fool!" The Colonel raised his clenched fists, his skin flushing, a wild light in his eyes. He still did not want to believe what had happened, possibly could not believe. The lieutenant was younger, a reserve officer; as much as he disliked it he could face the facts.

"Colonel, you must believe me. The situation is desperate, and desperate times call for desperate solutions . . ."

"*Sergeant*! Take this lieutenant and this civilian to the target range and shoot them for violating security during an emergency."

"Colonel, please . . ."

"Sergeant, that is an *order*!"

The Sergeant who was only four months short of retirement and had a pot belly to prove it, looked from one officer to the other. He was reluctant to make a decision but he had to. He finally rose and went to the toilet, locking the door behind him. The Colonel, who had been following his movements in eye-bulging silence, gasped, his face a bright scarlet, and groped for his sidearm. Even as he drew it from the holster he gurgled and fell face first upon the desk, then slid slowly to the floor.

"Medic!" the Lieutenant shouted and ran and opened the Colonel's collar. The medic took one look and shook his head gloomily. "The big one. He's had it. Always had a dicey ticker."

The Sergeant came out of the toilet and helped the Lieutenant to

HARRY HARRISON

HARRY HARRISON, author of *Bill the Galactic Hero,* a satire on the military, currently enjoys a reputation as one of the most popular writers on the SF scene. Born in Stanford, Connecticut in 1925 he has been an editor, anthologist, a cartoonist, a commercial illustrator and a machine-gun instructor during World War II.

In 1951 *Worlds Beyond* published his first SF story *Rod Diver* and he became a regular contributor to the magazine. Later he expanded the adventures of Jason din Ald, a character he had developed in his short stories, into the three novels which form the *Deathworld Trilogy*.

Harrison cavorts from the humour of his *Stainless Steel Rat* series, which tell of the adventures of Slippery Jim di-Griz, to the splendid combination of science fiction and fantasy of *A Transatlantic Tunnel, Hurrah* an "alternate world" story in which Britain and its colony America are to be linked by a tunnel under the Atlantic Ocean.

His novel *Make Room, Make Room*, a futuristic detective story set on an over-populated Earth where food is scarce was filmed as *Soylent Green* in 1973. Directed by Richard Fleischer, the production won a Nebula award in the same year.

***An Honest Day's Work* sees Harrison in a light mood as he weaves a story of an alien invasion thwarted by a most unlikely hero.**

pull a gas cape over the corpse. Jerry Cruncher stood to one side and looked on in silence, sucking on his pipe.

"Please, Mr. Cruncher," the Lieutenant said pleadingly, "you must help us. You're our last hope now."

* * *

Now when we look back at Black Sunday when the Disaster began, we can marvel at the simplicity of the Betelgeusean plan and understand why it came within a hair's breadth of succeeding. Our armies and space-borne tanks were poised and waiting, all instruments and attention firmly fixed on the massive bulk of the "so called" trade station which was, indeed, just a trade station. On Earth a complex spiderweb of communication networks linked together the host of defenders, a multi-level net of radio and laser links, buried coaxial cables and land lines, microwave and heliograph connections.

It was foolproof and unjammable and perfect in every way except for the fact that all global communications were channelled through the two substations and ComCent in Global City. These three stations, wonderfully efficient, handled all the communications with the armed forces on Earth, below the ground, on the Moon and in space.

They were knocked out. Betelgeusean commando squads in field armour dropped one null-G on to each centre and the battle could not have lasted more than half an hour. When it was over the three communications centres had been taken and the war was lost before it began. Headquarters were cut off from units, individual units from each other, tanks from tank commanders, spaceships from their bases. Radar central on the far side of the Moon very quickly discovered the blips of the invasion fleet swooping in from beyond Saturn. But there was no way they could tell anyone about it.

* * *

"I have to ask my supervisor about it," Jerry Cruncher said, nodding solemnly at the thought. "This being my day off and all. And taking of unauthorised people into the tunnels. Can't say he's going to like it much."

"Mr. Cruncher," the Lieutenant said through tight-clamped teeth. "In case you have not heard, there is a war on. You have just seen a man die because of this war. You cannot call your supervisor because the military override has rendered the civilian visiphone network inoperable."

"Can't say I like that."

"None of us do. That is why we need your help. The enemy aliens have taken our communication centres and they must be recaptured. We have contacted the nearest combat unit by messenger and they are attempting to retake the centre, but they are virtually impregnable."

"They are? How did those Beetlejuicians capture them then?"

"Well, yes, it is Sunday, you know, minimum personnel, at 0800 hours the church coaches were leaving, the gates were open . . ."

"Caught you with your pants down, hey?" A wet suck on his pipe told the world what Jerry Cruncher felt about that kind of efficiency. "So your lot is out and you want back in. So why bother a working man at home on a Sunday?"

"Because, Mr. Cruncher, war does not recognise days of the week. And you are the oldest employee of CitSubMaint and probably the only man who can answer this question. Our communication centres have their own standby power sources, but they normally use city power. And the land lines and cables go out underground. Now, think carefully before you answer, can we get into these centres from underground? Particularly into ComCent?"

"Where is it?" He tamped down the glowing tobacco with a calloused thumb, then sucked in the grey smoke happily.

"At the junction of 18th Way and Wiggan Road."

"So *that's* why there are so many cables in 104-BpL."

"*Can* we get into it?"

In the hushed silence that followed the burble of Jerry Cruncher's pipe could be clearly heard. The Lieutenant stood, fists clenched tightly, and beside him the Sergeant and the Corpsman, as well as the operators who had left their silent communication equipment. All of them waited and listened in strained silence as Jerry Cruncher narrowed his eyes in thought, took the pipe from his mouth and exhaled a cloud of pungent smoke, then turned to face them.

"Yep," he said.

They weren't the best troops – but they were troops. Technicians and operators, MPs and cooks, clerks, and motor pool mechanics. But they were armed with the best weapons the armouries could provide and armoured as well with a sense of purpose. If they stood a little straighter or held their guns a little more firmly it was because they knew that the future of the world was in their hands. They marched with grim precision to the road junction where they had been instructed to wait and had been there no more than a few minutes when Jerry Cruncher showed up.

He wore waterproofs and a hardhat, heavy gumboots that came to his waist, while a worn and ancient toolbox was slung by a strap over one shoulder. His pipe was out, but still clamped in his jaw, as he moved his shrewd eyes over the waiting troops.

"Not dressed right," he said.

"Everyone is in combat uniform," the Lieutenant answered.

"Not right for the tunnels. Gets mighty damp . . ."

"Mr. Cruncher, these are volunteer soldiers. They may die for their world so they do not mind getting wet for it. May we go now?"

Shaking his head in solemn disapproval Jerry Cruncher led the way to a manhole in the road, into the socket of which he inserted a shining tool with which, in a practised movement, he flipped the heavy manhole lid aside.

"Follow me then, single file. Last two men in slide that lid back on and watch out for your fingers. Here we go."

Automatic lights sprang on as they climbed down the ladder to the cool, green tunnel below. Wires, cables and pipes lined the walls and ceiling in a maze that only a Jerry Cruncher could make head or tail of. He slapped them affectionately as they passed.

"Water main, steam main, 50,000 volt line, 220 local feeder, telephone, teletype, co-ax, ice water, pneumo-delivery, food dispenser supply, oxygen, sewer feeder." He chuckled happily, "Yep, we've got a little bit of everything down here."

"Medic!" a voice called from the rear of the file and the Corpsman hurried away.

"They've found us!" A Permanent KP wailed and there was a rattle of weapons readied.

"Put those away!" the Lieutenant shouted. "Before you kill each other. Get me a report, Sergeant, snap to it."

They waited, weapons clenched and eyes rolling with anxiety, until the Sergeant returned. Jerry Cruncher hummed to himself tonelessly as he tapped various valves with a small ballpean hammer, then carefully tightened the gasket retainer on one.

"Nothing much," the Sergeant said. "Burne-Smith got a finger mashed putting the lid back on."

"They never listen," Jerry Cruncher coughed disapprovingly.

"Move it out," the Lieutenant ordered.

"One thing we haven't mentioned," Jerry Cruncher said, unmoving as a block of stone. "You guaranteed that my supervisor would see that I received my pay for this job."

"Yes, of course, can we talk about it as we go?"

"We go when this is settled. I forgot that this being Sunday I'll be getting double time and triple after four hours."

"Fine, agreed. Let's go."

"In writing."

"Yes, writing, of course." The Lieutenant's scriber flew over a message pad and he ripped off the sheet. "There, I've signed it as well, with my serial number. The Army will stand behind this."

"Had better," Jerry Cruncher said, carefully folding the slip and placing it securely in his wallet before they moved out again.

It was a nightmare journey for all except the grey, solid man who led them like a Judas goat through this underground inferno. The main tunnels were easy enough to pass through, though pendant valvewheels and transverse pipes lay constantly in wait for the unwary. Had they not been wearing helmets half of the little force would have been stunned before they had gone a mile. As it was there was many a clank and muffled cry from the rear.

Then came the inspection hatch and the first crawltube leading to a vertical pit 60 feet deep, down which they had to make their way on a water-slippery ladder. At its foot an even damper tunnel, this one faced with blocks of hand-hewn stone, led them through the darkness – no lights here, they had to use their torches – to an immense cavern filled with roaring sound.

"Storm sewer," Jerry Cruncher said, pointing to the rushing river that swirled by just below their feet, "I've seen it bone dry in the season. Been rain in the suburbs lately, and here it is now. Stay on the walkway, this is the shortest way to go, and don't slip. Once in that water you're a goner. Might find your body 50 miles out in the ocean if the fishes don't get it first."

With this cheering encouragement the men slithered and crawled the awful length of that great tunnel, almost gasping with relief when they were back in the safety of a communications tube again. Shortly after this Jerry Cruncher halted and pointed up at a ladder that rose into the darkness above.

"98 BaG dropwell. This is the one you want, to that second centre you talked about."

"You're sure?"

Jerry Cruncher eyed the Lieutenant with something very much like disgust and he groped his pipe from his pocket.

"Being you're ignorant, mister, I take no offence. When Jerry says a tunnel is a tunnel, that's the tunnel he says."

"No offence meant!"

"None taken," he muttered around the pipe stem. "This is the one. You can see all the wires and communication cables going up there as well. Can't be anything else."

"What's at the top?"

"Door with a handle and a sign saying NO ADMISSION UNDER PAR. 897A OF THE MILITARY CODE."

"Is the door locked?"

"Nope. Forbidden under paragraph 45-C of the Tunnel Authority Code. Need access, we do."

"Then this is it. Sergeant, take 18 men and get up that ladder. Synchronise your watch with mine. In two hours we go in. Just get through that door and start shooting – watch out for the equipment though – and keep shooting until every one of those slimy, dirty Betelgeuseans is dead. Do you understand?"

The Sergeant nodded with grim determination and drew himself up and saluted. "We'll do our duty, sir."

"All right, the rest of you, move out."

They had walked for no more than 10 minutes down a lateral tunnel lined with frosted pipes before Jerry Cruncher stopped and sat down.

"What's wrong?" the Lieutenant asked.

"Tea break," he said, putting his still warm pipe into his side pocket and opening his lunch box.

"You can't – I mean, listen, the enemy, the schedule . . ."

"I always have tea at this time." He poured a great mugful of the potent brew and sniffed it appreciatively. "Tea break allowed for in the schedule."

Most of the men brought out rations and sipped from their canteens while the Lieutenant paced back and forth slapping his fist into his hand. Jerry Cruncher sipped his tea placidly and chewed on a large chocolate biscuit.

A shrill scream sliced through the silence and echoed from the pipes.

Something black and awful launched itself from a crevice in the wall and was attached to Trooper Barnes' throat. The soldiers were paralysed. Not so Jerry Cruncher. There was a whistle and a thud as he instantly lashed out with his spanner and the vicious assailant rolled, dead, on to the tunnel floor before their bulging eyes.

"It's . . . it's . . . *hideous*!" a soldier gasped. "What is it?"

"Mutant hamster," Jerry Cruncher said as he picked up the monster of teeth and claws and stuffed it into his lunch box. "Descendants of house pets that escaped centuries ago, mutated here in the darkness until they turned into this. I've seen bigger ones. Boffins at the university give me three credits for every one I bring them. Not bad if I say so myself, and tax free too, which I hope you won't be repeating."

He was almost jovial now at this fiscally remunerative encounter. As soon as the trooper had been sewn up they pressed on.

A second squad was left at the next communication substation and they hurried on towards ComCent itself.

"Ten minutes to go," the Lieutenant gasped, jogging heavily under the weight of all his equipment.

"Not to worry, just two tunnels more."

It was three minutes to deadline when they reached the wide opening in the ceiling above them, sprouting cables from its mouth like an electronic hydra's head.

"Big door at the top," Jerry Cruncher said, shining his torch up the shaft. "Has a dual interlock compound wheel exchange lever. As you turn the wheel counterclockwise the lever in position *ready* must be . . ."

"Come up with us, please," the Lieutenant begged, peering at his watch and chewing his lip nervously. "We'll never get in in time and they'll be warned by the attacks on the other stations."

"Not my job, you know, getting shot at. I let them as has been paid for it do it."

"Please, I beg of you, as a patriotic citizen." Jerry Cruncher's face was as of carved stone as he bit down heavily on the stem of his pipe. "You owe it to yourself, your family, your conscience, your country. And I can guarantee a 100 credit bonus for opening it."

"Done."

They climbed against time and when they reached the platform at the top, the second hand on the Lieutenant's watch was just coming up on the 12.

"Open it!"

The wheel spun and gears engaged, the great lever went down and the massive portal swung open.

"For Mother Earth!" the Lieutenant shouted and led the charge.

When they had all gone inside and the tunnel was silent again Jerry Cruncher lit his pipe and then, more out of curiosity than anything else, strolled in after them. It was a vista of endless steel corridors lined with banks of instruments, whirring and humming under electronic control.

He stopped to tamp down his pipe just as a door opened and a short hairy creature, no taller than his waist, shaped like a bowling pin and

possessing a number of arms, scuttled out and raced towards a large red switch mounted on the opposite wall. Five of its arms were reaching for the switch, spatulate fingers almost touching it, when the spanner whistled once again and sank deep into the creature's head, flooring it instantly, Jerry Cruncher had just retrieved the spanner when the white-faced Lieutenant raced through the same door.

"Praise heaven!" he gasped, "you've stopped him in time."

"Didn't like his looks at all, though I didn't mean to bash his brains in."

"That is their leader, the only survivor, and he was going for the destruct switch that would have blown us all a mile high. He's our prisoner now and he'll talk, believe me. You didn't kill him. The Betelgeuseans have their brains in their midriffs, their stomachs are in their heads. He's just unconscious."

"Like a boot in the guts. Glad of that, didn't mean to kill him."

* * *

"Where you been?" Agatha called from the kitchen when she heard Jerry's heavy tread in the hall.

"Special job," he wheezed, pulling off his high boots. "Going to be some extra lolly in the pay packet this week."

"We'll need it to fix the viddy. It's been out of order all day, though it just came back on. Something wrong with it I'm sure. Had phone trouble too, would you believe, all in the same day. Tried to call Mum but our line went dead. Was it a hard job?"

"Not specially," Jerry grunted, digging out his pipe. "Government work, bit of a bonus in it too I imagine. Showed a bunch of chaps through the tunnels. Not a clue they had. One mashed his hand in a lid and the other just sat there while a hampmutey went for this throat."

"Oooh, don't say that, I'll have no appetite at all. Tea's ready."

"Now *that* is the sort of thing I like to hear."

He smiled for the first time since he had got out of bed that morning and went in to have his tea.

Action replay

BY RICHARD QUARRIE

THE BALL ROCKETED INTO THE BACK OF THE NET. Geoff Harrison gave a low whistle of appreciation. No matter how many times he saw the playback there was always that same surging thrill, that quickening of the pulse.

"I think we'll have that one again, Prince."

Prince opened one sleepy eye as Geoff pressed the switch on the video-recording machine, letting the tape run backwards for a couple of minutes.

"Should be about right, old son. What a pity you can't appreciate Ricardo Villa's goal."

Geoff started the tape running again, settling back in his chair to savour one of the highlights of the football year. The video had arrived just in time to record the Replay of the F.A. Cup Final, and with Frances out at the pictures he had a whole evening to re-live Spurs' victory.

The TV screen flickered into life again. As the picture formed Geoff shot up in his chair with a gasp of surprise, the sudden movement drawing a protesting growl from the labrador lying at his feet. For once Geoff had no thought for the dog. For the scene which met his astonished gaze was not the emerald-green turf of Wembley stadium. Instead there stretched away into the distance a long vista of neat little terrace houses; dark weathered brickwork, white window frames, slate-grey roofs, each stone step sanded to perfection; only the colours of the doors and the different patterns of net curtaining reflecting the taste of the occupants.

The figure of a small boy ran up to one of the doors, cap on one side of his head, his hand clutching a small brown envelope. As he stood on tiptoes to turn its handle the door opened. The ample figure of a woman in a white pinafore reached down to greet the boy, taking the envelope from him. Reading its contents quickly, she threw her arms around him, enfolding him in an embrace that was warm and loving.

Geoff felt a prick of tears behind the eyes as he saw his boyhood self and his mother on that never-to-be-forgotten day when he had finished top of the class. How thrilled his mother had been. How great his own joy at having pleased her. As he stared at the screen, moved to the depths of his being by the memory, the picture changed. The goal he had seen a few moments before thudded once more into the netting.

Geoff leaned forward and switched off the machine, staring at the blank face of the TV set, his mind racing. He cast a quick glance round the semi-darkened room. At the familiar books and furniture; the now-silent television; Prince, stretching and yawning beside his chair; the glass of whisky-and-water on the table beside him. Everything *seemed* normal. Yet the hand he reached out to take the glass trembled a little.

Trying hard to calm down he took a large draught of the whisky. Could it have been a trick of the imagination? A fond memory from the past strong enough to cut across the thoughts and actions of the present? He had certainly been overworking lately and there was that nagging worry in the back of his mind about Frances again. He sighed. What a pity that life hadn't always been as happy as in those early days. Yet it had not all been bad. There had been some good moments.

He pressed the switch again expecting the football game to continue. The picture began to form and spread across the screen. The turf was every bit as green as at Wembley, but the game was one of white shirts and flannels. Geoff felt a tingle at the back of his neck as he recognised the slim, young figure at the crease. As soon as the ball left the bowler's arm he knew exactly what was to come. The hard, leather missile hurtled down the pitch straight on to the bat. A deft turn of the wrists and it sped off to the boundary. He saw himself turn away from the wicket heading towards the pavilion amid the thunderous acclaim of his school-fellows. That was the winning hit which brought the Senior Cup to his school for the first time.

Geoff switched off hurriedly. Then poured himself another measure of whisky. Swallowing it quickly, the fiery liquid burned the back of his throat. He ejected the tape from the machine, examining it closely by the light of the reading lamp. There was nothing to indicate that it was anything other than the tape he had recorded only last Thursday. The Cup Final label was the one he had printed in his own neat hand. And yet, if he could believe his eyes, it had thrown up two vivid moments from his past. Could there be more? If there was *did he really want to see it?*

Geoff hesitated then slipped the tape back into the machine and switched on. He let the tape run without vision until about half-way through its length before stopping it and bringing the picture on to the screen. He was relieved to see that it was the closing moment of the first half. The whistle blew. The players ran off to their dressing rooms and the camera panned across to pick them up. As the last of them disappeared down the tunnel two figures rose up out of the darkness. Emerging hand in hand, the dazzling white of her wedding gown contrasting sharply with the dark grey of his suit, Frances and he stood on the porch of the church where they had just been married.

"God, how beautiful she looked," Geoff heard himself saying, the football game now forgotten. The dog stirred restlessly under his hand as the tremor of his fingers transferred his unease to the animal. Geoff watched, eyes fixed on the screen, as Frances turned her head towards him, saw his own head come down to hers, felt the physical shock of the kiss as their lips met. He felt himself reliving the whole, wonderful sensation of that moment through the medium of the TV screen. He had no idea why it should be happening. All he knew was that the incredible

video-machine had picked out those memorable experiences and played them back to him for his delight.

Could there be more magic in store?

Geoff was sitting bolt upright now. A cold trickle of sweat ran down inside the neck-band of his shirt. He let the tape run on. One by one the pictures came up on the screen uninterrupted now by any of the action from Wembley stadium. The video-tape had taken over and Geoff had no wish to stop it.

There was the first stupid row he'd had with Frances, the angry words, the tears, the making-up afterwards which had almost made the row worth while. Then the time he had lost his job. On the scrap-heap for a whole year. Frances had gone out to work to make ends meet. The terrible scenes of jealousy which followed when she had started coming home late, when it was all too apparent that she had found other interests. Geoff could feel the stab of pain even now.

But that was all over, surely. A thing of the past. He leaned forward and switched off the machine. It was only then that he felt the tension in Prince's body, heard the low frightened growl from the animal.

"You too, old pal?"

Geoff ran a nervous hand through the wiry greyness of his hair. Should he go on? The machine seemed to have got into a depressing groove intent now on replaying some of the darker moments of his life, he could sense the air of unease which pervaded the room. What had started as fun now bordered on terror. *The terror of a machine which he could no longer control.*

Yet, if it should be on tape, there was that lovely reconciliation with Frances still to come. When she made the promise that from now on things would be different.

He had to see it through.

He switched on.

It was all there just as he had anticipated. Right up to the time earlier this evening when Frances had closed the door behind her as she went off to the cinema. Thinking it was the end of the tape he reached out to switch off. His hand stopped midway towards the control.

The picture was running on. The door to the living-room had opened again. Frances and a man whose face was familiar were framed in the opening, their features picked out clearly in the light from the hall. Geoff racked his brain to remember where he had seen the man before. Then it came with a rush, *Jack Flynn.*

Frances had been head-over-heels in love with him before Geoff had come along and snatched her away from under Jack's very nose. His own image rose to its feet, turning towards the two figures in the doorway. Geoff saw his own startled look of surprise as the two rushed at him. The weapon in Flynn's hand struck first, sending him down on to the floor of the living-room, a pool of blood spreading across the carpet from a gaping head wound.

The picture faded.

Geoff found himself staring at its blankness, the whole of his body trembling, a terrible fear thrusting all reason out of his mind. Prince had fled into a corner, his head thrown back, a hideous growling rising from the depths of his throat.

He passed a hand across his brow, wiping the sweat away from his eyes. The machine had stopped of its own accord, but the growling of the dog and his own breathing broke the stillness of the room.

The click of the key being inserted in the front door lock sent another stabbing shock through Geoff's brain. He started to his feet. Perhaps the nightmare would end as soon as he saw Frances. Unless she had someone with her. He heard her gasp as she switched on the main light.

"Why, whatever's the matter. You're as white as a sheet. And what's up with the dog? You haven't been watching one of those old horror-movies again? I thought you were going to watch the football."

Geoff stared at his wife. A surge of relief welled up inside him as he realised she was alone. The whole thing must have been the product of an overwrought mind.

"No . . . no, love. It was just that . . . ," he stopped. "I've had a bit of a bad turn, that's all. It doesn't matter."

Frances appeared to be all concern. She put her arms round him briefly, but it was a gesture without any passion.

"Look, you'd better sit down. I'll go and make a cup of coffee."

Geoff sat back in his chair. He was beginning to feel silly, he knew he could never tell Frances about the tape, or his own imaginings. She would think he was crazy. Or making it up. He could hear her voice now, prattling on in the kitchen. Something about the film she had seen. Suddenly she caught his attention.

". . . and what do you know? You'll never guess who I bumped into after all these years. Jack Flynn. You remember him, don't you? One of my old flames. Says he'd like to come round and see you some night, and have a drink for old times' sake. You don't mind, do you, Geoff? Not after all this time. Well, Geoff? Geoff . . .?

The yellow pill

BY ROG PHILLIPS

DR. CEDRIC ELTON slipped into his office by the back entrance, took off his overcoat and hid it in the small, narrow-doored cupboard, then picked up the neatly piled patient cards his receptionist, Helena Fitzroy, had placed on the corner of his desk. There were only four, but there could have been a hundred if he had accepted everyone who asked to be his patient, because his successes had more than once been spectacular and his reputation as a psychiatrist had become so great because of this that his name had become synonymous with psychiatry in the public mind.

His eyes flicked over the top card. He frowned, then went to the small square of one-way glass in the reception-room door and looked through it. There were four police officers and a man in a strait jacket.

The card said the man's name was Gerald Bocek, and that he had shot and killed five people in a supermarket, and had killed one officer and wounded two others before being captured.

Except for the strait jacket, Gerald Bocek did not have the appearance of being dangerous. He was about 25, with brown hair and blue eyes. There were faint wrinkles of habitual good nature about his eyes. Right now he was smiling, relaxed, and idly watching Helena, who was pretending to study various cards in her desk file but was obviously conscious of her audience.

Cedric returned to his desk and sat down. The card for Jerry Bocek said more about the killings. When captured, Bocek insisted that the people he had killed were not people at all, but blue-scaled Venusian lizards who had boarded his spaceship, and that he had only been defending himself.

Dr. Cedric Elton shook his head in disapproval. Fantasy fiction was all right in its place, but too many people took it seriously. Of course, it was not the fault of the fiction. The same type of person took other types of fantasy seriously in earlier days, burning women as witches, stoning men as devils . . .

Abruptly Cedric deflected the control on the intercom and spoke into it. "Send Gerald Bocek in, please," he said.

A moment later the door to the reception-room opened. Helena flashed Cedric a scared smile and got out of the way quickly. One police officer led the way, followed by Gerald Bocek closely flanked by two officers with the fourth one in the rear, who carefully closed the door. It was impressive, Cedric decided. He nodded towards a chair in front of his desk and the police officers sat the strait-jacketed man in it, then hovered nearby, ready for anything.

"You're Jerry Bocek?" Cedric asked.

The strait-jacketed man nodded cheerfully.

"I'm Dr. Cedric Elton, a psychiatrist," Cedric said. "Do you have any idea at all why you have been brought to me?"

"Brought to you?" Jerry echoed, chuckling. "Don't kid me. You're my old pal, Gar Castle. Brought to you? How could I get *away* from you in this stinking tub?"

"Stinking tub?" Cedric said.

"Spaceship," Jerry said. "Look, Gar. Untie me, will you? This nonsense has gone far enough."

"My name is Dr. Cedric Elton," Cedric enunciated. "You are not on a spaceship. You were brought to my office by the four policemen standing behind you, and . . ."

Jerry Bocek turned his head and studied each of the four policemen with frank curiosity. "What policemen?" he interrupted. "You mean these four gear lockers?" He turned his head back and looked pityingly at Dr. Elton. "You'd better get hold of yourself, Gar," he said. "You're imagining things."

"My name is Dr. Cedric Elton," Cedric said.

Gerald Bocek leaned forward and said with equal firmness, "Your name is Gar Castle. I refuse to call you Dr. Cedric Elton because your name is Gar Castle, and I'm going to keep on calling you Gar Castle because we have to have at least one peg of rationality in all this madness or you will be cut completely adrift in this dream world you've cooked up."

Cedric's eyebrows shot halfway up to his hairline.

"Funny," he mused, smiling. "That's exactly what I was just going to say to you!"

* * *

Cedric continued to smile. Jerry's serious intenseness slowly faded. Finally an answering smile tugged at the corners of his mouth. When it became a grin Cedric laughed, and Jerry began to laugh with him. The four police officers looked at one another uneasily.

"Well!" Cedric finally gasped. "I guess that puts us on an even footing! You're nuts to me and I'm nuts to you!"

"An equal footing is right!" Jerry shouted in high glee. Then abruptly he sobered. "Except," he said gently, "I'm tied up."

"In a strait jacket," Cedric corrected.

"Ropes," Jerry said firmly.

"You're dangerous," Cedric said. "You killed six people, one of them a police officer, and wounded two other officers."

"I blasted five Venusian lizard pirates who boarded our ship," Jerry said, "and melted the door from one food locker, and seared the paint on two others. You know as well as I do, Gar, how space madness causes you to personify everything. That's why they drill into you that the minute you think there are more people on board the ship than there were at the beginning of the trip you'd better go to the medicine locker and take a yellow pill.

"They can't hurt anything but a delusion."

"If that is so," Cedric said, "why are *you* in a strait jacket?"

"I'm tied up with ropes," Jerry said patiently. "You tied me up. Remember?"

"And those four police officers behind you are gear lockers?" Cedric said. "O.K., if one of those gear lockers comes around in front of you and taps you on the jaw with his fist, would you still believe it's a gear locker?"

Cedric nodded to one of the officers, and the man came around in front of Gerald Bocek and, quite carefully, hit him hard enough to rock his head but not hurt him. Jerry's eyes blinked with surprise, then he looked at Cedric and smiled.

"Did you feel that?" Cedric said quietly.

"Feel what?" Jerry said. "Oh!" He laughed. "You imagined that one of the gear lockers – a police officer in your dream world – came around in front of me and hit me?" He shook his head in pity. "Don't you understand, Gar, that it didn't really happen? Untie me and I'll prove it. Before your very eyes I'll open the door on your *Policeman* and take out the pressure suit, or magnetic grapple, or whatever is in it. Or are you afraid to? You've surrounded yourself with all sorts of protective delusions. I'm tied with ropes, but you imagine it to be a strait jacket. You imagine yourself to be a psychiatrist named Dr. Cedric Elton, so that you can convince yourself that you're sane and I'm crazy. Probably you imagine yourself a very *famous* psychiatrist that everyone would like to come to for treatment. World famous, no doubt. Probably you even think you have a beautiful receptionist? What is her name?"

"Helena Fitzroy," Cedric said.

Jerry nodded. "It figures," he said resignedly. "Helena Fitzroy is the Expediter at Marsport. You try to date her every time we land there, but she won't date you."

"Hit him again," Cedric said to the officer. While Jerry's head was still rocking from the blow, Cedric said, "Now! Is it *my* imagination that your head is still rocking from the blow?"

"What blow?" Jerry said, smiling serenely. "I felt no blow."

"Do you mean to say," Cedric said incredulously, "that there is no corner of your mind, no slight residue of rationality, that tries to tell you your rationalisations aren't reality?"

Jerry smiled ruefully. "I have to admit," he said, "when you seem so absolutely certain you're right and I'm nuts, its almost makes me doubt. Untie me, Gar, and let's try to work this thing out sensibly." He grinned. "You know, Gar, *one* of us has to be nuttier than a fruit cake."

"If I had the officers take off your strait jacket, what would you do?" Cedric asked. "Try to grab a gun and kill some more people?"

"That's one of the things I'm worried about," Jerry said. "If those pirates came back, with me tied up, you're just space crazy enough to

ROG PHILLIPS

"ROG PHILLIPS" was a pseudonym of Roger Phillips Graham, born in 1909 at Spokane, Washington.

He attended the universities of Washington and Gonzaga studying mathematics. During the late 1940's he contributed many short stories to the American "pulp" magazines and had a fan column in *Amazing*.

He wrote several novels, two memorable tales being *The Involuntary Immortals* and *Time Trap*. His stories have appeared in the *Best of SF* Anthologies.

In 1960 he entered the Mystery writing field, he was not to write fantasy fiction again. His new stories were regularly featured in the *Best Detective Stories* collections of the early 1960's.

His health was very bad and his writing not as prolific as in earlier years, although it was of a better quality. He died in 1966 leaving some 3,000,000 printed words to his credit.

***The Yellow Pill* was his last SF story, he had had the idea for two years, but finally had written the story in about five hours solid work. It is probably his finest tale in this field.**

welcome them aboard. That's why you *must* untie me. Our lives may depend on it, Gar."

"Where would you get a gun?" Cedric asked.

"Where they're always kept," Jerry said. "In the gear lockers."

Cedric looked at the four policemen, their revolvers holstered at their hips, and sighed. One of them grinned feebly at him.

"I'm afraid we can't take your strait jacket off just yet," Cedric said. "I'm going to have the officers take you back now. I'll talk with you again tomorrow. Meanwhile I want you to think seriously about things. Try to get below this level of rationalisation that walls you off from reality. Once you make a dent in it the whole delusion will vanish." He looked up at the officers. "All right, take him away. Bring him back the same time tomorrow."

The officers urged Jerry to his feet. Jerry looked down at Cedric, a gentle expression on his face. "I'll try to do that, Gar," he said. "And I hope you do the same thing. I'm much encouraged. Several times I detected genuine doubt in your eyes. And . . ." Two of the officers pushed him firmly towards the door. As they opened it Jerry turned his head and looked back. "*Take* one of those yellow pills in the medicine locker, Gar," he pleaded. "It can't hurt you."

* * *

At a little before 5.30 Cedric tactfully eased his last patient all the way across the reception-room and out, then locked the door and leaned his back against it.

"Today was rough," he sighed.

Helena glanced up at him briefly, then continued typing. "I only have a little more on this last transcript," she said.

A minute later she pulled the paper from the typewriter and placed it on the neat stack beside her.

"I'll sort and file them in the morning," she said. "It was rough, wasn't it, doctor? That Gerald Bocek is the most unusual patient you've had since I've worked for you. And poor Mr. Potts. A brilliant executive, making half a million a year, and he's going to give it up. He seems so normal."

"He is normal," Cedric said. "People with above normal blood pressure often have very minor cerebral haemorrhages so small that the affected area is no larger than the head of a pin. All that happens is that they completely forget things that they knew. They can relearn them, but a man whose judgment must always be perfect can't afford to take the chance. He's already made one error in judgment that cost his company a million and a half. That's why I consented to take him on as a – Gerald Bocek really upset me, Helena. I *consent* to take a 500,000 dollar a year executive as a patient."

"He was frightening, wasn't he," Helena said. "I don't mean so much because he's a mass murderer as . . ."

"I know. I know," Cedric said. "Let's prove him wrong. Have dinner with me."

"We agreed . . ."

"Let's break the agreement this once."

Helena shook her head firmly. "Especially not now," she said. "Besides, it wouldn't prove anything. He's got you boxed in on that point. If I went to dinner with you, it would only show that a wish fulfilment entered your dream world."

"Ouch," Cedric said, wincing. "That's a dirty word. I wonder how he knew about the yellow pills? I can't get out of my mind the fact that *if* we had spaceships and *if* there were a type of space madness in which you began to personify objects, a yellow pill would be the right thing to stop that."

"How?" Helena said.

"They almost triple the strength of nerve currents from end organs. What results is that reality practically shouts down any fantasy insertions. It's quite startling. I took one three years ago when they first became available. You'd be surprised how little you actually see of what you look at, especially of people. You look at symbol inserts instead. I had to cancel my appointments for a week. I found I couldn't work without my professionally built symbol inserts about people that enable me to see them – not as they really are – but as a complex of normal and abnormal symptoms."

"I'd like to take one sometime," Helena said.

"That's a twist," Cedric said, laughing. "One of the characters in a dream world takes a yellow pill and discovers it doesn't exist at all except as a fantasy."

"Why don't we both take one," Helena said.

"Uh uh," Cedric said firmly. "I couldn't do my work."

"You're afraid you might wake up on a spaceship?" Helena said, grinning.

"Maybe I am," Cedric said. "Crazy, isn't it? But there is one thing today that stands out as a serious flaw in my reality. It's so glaring that I actually am afraid to ask you about it."

"Are you serious?" Helena said.

"I am." Cedric nodded. "How does it happen that the police brought Gerald Bocek here to my office instead of holding him in the psychiatric ward at City Hospital and having me go there to see him? How does it happen the D.A. didn't get in touch with me beforehand and discuss the case with me?"

"I . . . I don't know!" Helena said. "I received no call. They just showed up, and I assumed they wouldn't have without your knowing about it and telling them to. Mrs. Fortesque was your first patient and I called her at once and caught her just as she was leaving the house, and told her an emergency case had come up." She looked at Cedric with round, startled eyes.

"Now we know how the patient must feel," Cedric said, crossing the reception-room to his office door. "Terrifying, isn't it, to think that if I took a yellow pill all this might *vanish* – my years of college, my internship, *my fame as the world's best known psychiatrist*, and you. Tell me, Helena, are you sure you aren't an Expediter at Marsport?"

He leered at her mockingly as he slowly closed the door, cutting off his view of her.

* * *

Cedric put his coat away and went directly to the small square of one-way glass in the reception-room door. Gerald Bocek, still in strait jacket, was there, and so were the same four police officers.

Cedric went to his desk and, without sitting down, deflected the control on the intercom.

"Helena," he said, "before you send in Gerald Bocek, get me the D.A. on the phone."

He glanced over the four patient cards while waiting. Once he rubbed his eyes gently. He had had a restless night.

When the phone rang he reached for it. "Hello? Dave?" he said. "About this patient, Gerald Bocek . . ."

"I was going to call you today," the District Attorney's voice sounded. "I called you yesterday morning at ten, but no one answered, and I haven't had time since. Our police psychiatrist, Walters, says you might be able to snap Bocek out of it in a couple of days – at least long enough so that we can get some sensible answers out of him.

"Down underneath his delusion of killing lizard pirates from Venus there has to be some reason for that mass killing, and the Press is after us on this."

"But why bring him to my office?" Cedric said. "It's O.K., of course, but . . . that is . . . I didn't think you could! Take a patient out of the ward at City Hospital and transport him around town."

"I thought that would be less of an imposition on you," the D.A. said. "I'm in a hurry on it."

"Oh," Cedric said. "Well, O.K., Dave. He's out in the waiting-room. I'll do my best to snap him back to reality for you."

He hung up slowly, frowning. '*Less of an imposition*!' His whispered words floated into his ears as he snapped into the intercom, "Send Gerald Bocek in, please."

The door from the reception-room opened, and once again the procession of patient and police officers entered.

"Well, well, good morning, Gar," Jerry said. "Did you sleep well? I could hear you talking to yourself most of the night."

"I am Dr. Cedric Elton," Cedric said firmly.

"Oh, yes," Jerry said. "I promised to try to see things your way, didn't I? I'll try to co-operate with you, Dr. Elton." Jerry turned to the four officers. "Let's see now, these gear lockers are policemen, aren't they. How do you do, officers." He bowed to them, then looked around him. "And," he said, "this is your office, Dr. Elton. A very impressive office. That thing you're sitting behind is not the chart table but your desk, I gather." He studied the desk intently. "All metal, with a grey finish, isn't it?"

"All wood," Cedric said. "Walnut."

"Yes, of course," Jerry murmured. "How stupid of me. I really want to get into your reality, Gar . . . I mean Dr. Elton. Or get you into mine. I'm the one who's at a disadvantage, though. Tied up, I can't get into the medicine locker and take a yellow pill like you can. Did you take one yet?"

"Not yet," Cedric said.

"Uh, why don't you describe your office to me, Dr. Elton?" Jerry said. "Let's make a game of it. Describe parts of things and then let me see if I can fill in the rest. Start with your desk. It's genuine walnut? An executive style desk. Go on from there."

"All right," Cedric said. "Over here to my right is the intercom, made of grey plastic. And directly in front of me is the telephone."

"Stop," Jerry said. "Let me see if I can tell you your telephone number." He leaned over the desk and looked at the telephone, trying to keep his balance in spite of his arms being encased in the strait jacket. "Hm-m-m," he said, frowning. "Is the number Mulberry 5–9037?"

"No," Cedric said. "It's Cedar sev . . ."

"Stop!" Jerry said. "Let me say it. It's Cedar 7–4399."

"So you did read it and were just having your fun," Cedric snorted.

"If you say so," Jerry said.

"What other explanation can you have for the fact that it is my number, if you're unable to actually see reality?" Cedric said.

"You're absolutely right, Dr. Elton," Jerry said. "I think I understand the tricks my mind is playing on me now. I read the number on your phone, but it didn't enter my awareness. Instead, it cloaked itself with the pattern of my delusion, so that consciously I pretended to look at a phone that I couldn't see, and I thought, 'His phone number will obviously be one he's familiar with'. The most probable is the home phone of Helena Fitzroy in Marsport, so I gave you that, but it wasn't it.

When you said Cedar I knew right away it was your own apartment phone number."

Cedric sat perfectly still. Mulberry 5–9037 was actually Helena's apartment phone number. He hadn't recognised it until Gerald Bocek told him.

"Now you're beginning to understand," Cedric said after a moment. "Once you realise that your mind has walled off your consciousness from reality, and is substituting a rationalised pattern of symbology in its place, it shouldn't be long until you break through. Once you manage to see one thing as it really is, the rest of the delusion will disappear."

"I understand now," Jerry said gravely. "Let's have some more of it. Maybe I'll catch on."

They spent an hour at it. Towards the end Jerry was able to finish the descriptions of things with very little error.

"You are definitely beginning to get through," Cedric said with enthusiasm.

Jerry hesitated. "I suppose so," he said. "I must. But on the conscious level I have the idea – a rationalisation, of course – that I am beginning to catch on to the pattern of your imagination so that when you give me one or two key elements I can fill in the rest. But I'm going to try, really try – Dr. Elton."

"Fine," Cedric said heartily. "I'll see you tomorrow, same time. We should make the break-through then."

When the four officers had taken Gerald Bocek away, Cedric went into the outer office.

"Cancel the rest of my appointments," he said.

"But why?" Helena protested.

"Because I'm upset!" Cedric said. "How did a madman whom I never knew until yesterday know your phone number?"

"He could have looked it up in the phone book," Helena said.

"Locked in a room in the psychiatric ward at City Hospital?" Cedric said. "How did he know your name yesterday?"

"Why," Helena said, "all he had to do was read it on my desk here."

Cedric looked down at the brass name-plate.

"Yes," he grunted. "Of course. I'd forgotten about that. I'm so accustomed to it being there that I never see it."

He turned abruptly and went back into his office.

He sat down at his desk, then got up and went into the sterile whiteness of his compact laboratory. Ignoring the impressive battery of electronic instruments he went to the medicine cabinet. Inside, on the top shelf, was the glass-stoppered bottle he wanted. Inside it were a hundred vivid yellow pills. He shook out one and put the bottle away, then went back into his office. He sat down, placing the yellow pill in the centre of the white notepad.

There was a brief knock on the door to the reception-room and the door opened. Helena came in.

"I've cancelled all your other appointments for today," she said. "Why don't you go out to the golf course? A change will do you . . ." She saw the yellow pill in the centre of the white notepad and stopped.

"Why do you look so frightened?" Cedric said. "Is it because, if I take this little yellow pill, you'll cease to exist?"

"Don't joke," Helena said.

"I'm not joking," Cedric said. "Out there, when you mentioned about your brass name-plate on your desk, when I looked down it was blurred for just a second, then became sharply distinct and solid. And into my head popped the memory that the first thing I do when I have to get a new receptionist is get a brass name-plate for her and when she quits I make her a present of it."

"But that's the truth," Helena said. "You told me all about it when I started working for you. You also told me that while you still had your reason about you I was to solemnly promise that I would never accept an invitation from you for dinner or anything else, because business could not mix with pleasure. Do you remember that?"

"I remember," Cedric said. "A nice pat rationalisation in any man's reality to make the rejection be my own before you could have time to reject me yourself. Preserving the ego is the first principle of madness."

"But it isn't!" Helena said. "Oh, darling, I'm *here*! This is *real*! I don't care if you fire me or not. I've loved you forever, and you mustn't let that mass murderer get you down. I actually think he isn't insane at all, but has just figured out a way to seem insane so he won't have to pay for his crime."

"You think so?" Cedric said, interested. "It's a possibility. But he would have to be as good a psychiatrist as I am – You see? Delusions of grandeur."

"Sure," Helena said, laughing thinly. "Napoleon was obviously insane because he thought he was Napoleon."

"Perhaps," Cedric said. "But you must admit that if you are real, my taking this yellow pill isn't going to change that, but only confirm the fact."

"And make it impossible for you to do your work for a week," Helena said.

"A small price to pay for sanity," Cedric said. "No, I'm going to take it."

"You aren't!" Helena said, reaching for it.

Cedric picked it up an instant before she could get it. As she tried to get it away from him he evaded her and put it in his mouth. A loud gulp showed he had swallowed it.

He sat back and looked up at Helena curiously.

"Tell me, Helena," he said gently. "Did you know all the time that you were only a creature of my imagination? The reason I want to know is . . ."

He closed his eyes and clutched his head in his hands.

"God!" he groaned. "I feel like I'm dying! I didn't feel like this the first time I took one." Suddenly his mind steadied, and his thoughts cleared. He opened his eyes.

On the chart table in front of him the bottle of yellow pills lay on its side, pills scattered all over the table. On the other side of the control-room lay Jerry Bocek, his back propped against one of the four gear lockers, sound asleep, with so many ropes wrapped around him that it would probably be impossible for him to stand up.

Against the far wall were three other gear lockers, two of them with their paint badly scorched, the third with its door half melted off.

And in various positions about the control-room were the half charred bodies of five blue-scaled Venusian lizards.

A dull ache rose in Gar's chest. Helena Fitzroy was gone. Gone, when she had just confessed she loved him.

Unbidden, a memory came into Gar's mind. Dr. Cedric Elton was the psychiatrist who had examined him when he got his pilot's licence for third-class freighters . . .

"God!" Gar groaned again. And suddenly he was sick. He made a dash for the bathroom, and after a while he felt better.

When he straightened up from the wash-basin he looked at his reflection in the mirror for a long time, clinging to his hollow cheeks and sunken eyes. He must have been out of his head for two or three days. three days.

The first time. Awful! Somehow, he had never quite believed in space madness.

Suddenly he remembered Jerry. Poor Jerry!

Gar lurched from the bathroom back into the control-room. Jerry was awake. He looked up at Gar, forcing a smile to his lips.

"Hello, Dr. Elton," Jerry said.

Gar stopped as though shot.

"It's happened, Dr. Elton, just as you said it would," Jerry said, his smile widening.

"Forget that," Gar growled. "I took a yellow pill. I'm back to normal again."

Jerry's smile vanished abruptly. "I know what I did now," he said. "It's terrible. I killed six people. But I'm sane now. I'm willing to take what's coming to me."

"Forget that!" Gar snarled. "You don't have to humour me now. Just a minute and I'll untie you."

"Thanks, doctor," Jerry said. "It will sure be a relief to get out of this strait jacket."

Gar knelt beside Jerry and untied the knots in the ropes and unwound them from around Jerry's chest and legs.

"You'll be all right in a minute," Gar said, massaging Jerry's limp arms. The physical and nervous strain of sitting there immobilised had been rough. Slowly he worked circulation back into Jerry, then helped him to his feet.

"You don't need to worry, Dr. Elton," Jerry said. "I don't know why I killed those people, but I know I would never do such a thing again. I must have been insane."

"Can you stand now?" Gar said, letting go of Jerry.

Jerry took a few steps back and forth, unsteadily at first, then with better co-ordination. His resemblance to a robot decreased with exercise.

Gar was beginning to feel sick again. He fought it.

"You O.K. now, Jerry boy?" he asked worriedly.

"I'm fine now, Dr. Elton," Jerry said. "And thanks for everything you've done for me."

Abruptly Jerry turned and went over to the air-lock door and opened it.

"Good-bye now, Dr. Elton," he said.

"Wait!" Gar screamed, leaping towards Jerry.

But Jerry had stepped into the air-lock and closed the door. Gar tried to open it; but Jerry had already turned on the pump that would evacuate the air from the lock.

Screaming Jerry's name senselessly in horror, Gar watched through the small square of thick glass in the door as Jerry's chest quickly expanded, then collapsed as a mixture of phlegm and blood dribbled from his nostrils and lips, and his eyes enlarged and glazed over, then one of them ripped open and collapsed, its fluid draining down his cheek.

He watched as Jerry glanced towards the side of the air-lock and smiled, then spun the wheel that opened the air-lock to the vacuum of space, and stepped out.

And when Gar finally stopped screaming and sank to the deck, sobbing, his knuckles were broken and bloody from pounding on bare metal.

Great Lost Discoveries — III

Immortality

BY FREDRIC BROWN

THE THIRD GREAT DISCOVERY made and lost in the 20th-century was the secret of immortality. It was the discovery of an obscure Moscow chemist named Ivan Ivanovitch Smetakovsky, in 1978. Smetakovsky left no record of how he made his discovery or of how he knew before trying it that it would work, for the simple fact that it scared him stiff, for two reasons.

He was afraid to give it to the world, and he knew that once he had given it even to his own government the secret would eventually leak through the "Curtain" and cause chaos. The U.S.S.R. could handle anything, but in the more barbaric and less disciplined countries the inevitable result of an immortality drug would be a population explosion that would most assuredly lead to an attack on the enlightened Communist countries.

And he was afraid to take it himself because he wasn't sure he *wanted* to become immortal. With things as they were even in the U.S.S.R. – not to

FREDRIC BROWN

THE great humorist of science fiction, Fredric William Brown was born in 1906 in Cincinnati, Ohio. He was first employed as an office boy by a firm of machine-tool suppliers, and later became a proofreader for a printer.

He wrote both science fiction and detective stories throughout his career and became well-known as an author of short stories with twisted endings.

He is especially remembered for the maturity and humour of his stories.

His *What Mad Universe* was a brilliant satire on readers and writers of science fiction and is often considered his best work.

The little green men of *Martians Go Home* are completely different from those imagined by H.G. Wells, but they are just as disruptive—watching and commenting on *everything* we humans do.

Brown's serious side was represented by his novel *The Lights In The Sky Are Stars*. He died in 1972 in Tucson, Arizona.

In *Great Lost Discoveries I, II & III*, Fredric Brown demonstrates that a great wit doesn't need many pages to tell a funny tale. In fact he is the author of the shortest SF story ever written. Here it is in full:

"After the last atomic war, Earth was dead; nothing grew, nothing lived. The last man sat alone in a room. There was a knock on the door . . ."

consider what they must be outside it – was it really worth while to live forever or even indefinitely?

He compromised by neither giving it to anyone else nor taking it himself, for the time being, until he could make up his mind about it.

Meanwhile he carried with him the only dose of the drug he had made up. It was only a minute quantity that fitted into a tiny capsule that was insoluble and could be carried in his mouth. He attached it to the side of one of his dentures, so that it rested safely between denture and cheek and he would be in no danger of swallowing it inadvertently.

But if he should so decide at any time he could reach into his mouth, crush the capsule with a thumbnail, and become immortal.

He so decided one day when, after coming down with lobar pneumonia and being taken to a Moscow hospital, he learned from overhearing a conversation between a doctor and nurse who erroneously thought he was asleep, that he was expected to die within a few hours.

Fear of death proved greater than fear of immortality, whatever immortality might bring, so, as soon as the doctor and the nurse had left the room, he crushed the capsule and swallowed its contents.

He hoped that, since death might be so imminent, the drug would work in time to save his life. It did work in time, although by the time it had taken effect he had slipped into semicoma and delirium.

Three years later, in 1981, he was still in semicoma and delirium, and the Russian doctors had finally diagnosed his case and ceased to be puzzled by it.

Obviously Smetakovsky had taken some sort of immortality drug – one which they found it impossible to isolate or analyse – and it was keeping him from dying and would no doubt do so indefinitely if not forever.

But unfortunately it had also made immortal the pneumococci in his body, the bacteria (*Diplococci pneumoniae*) that had caused his pneumonia in the first place and would continue to maintain it forever. So the doctors, being realists and seeing no reason to burden themselves by giving him custodial care in perpetuity, simply buried him.

The Nothing

BY FRANK HERBERT

IF IT HADN'T BEEN FOR THE FIGHT with my father I'd never have gone down to the Tavern and then I wouldn't have met the *Nothing*. This *Nothing* was really just an ordinary looking guy. He wasn't worth special attention unless, like me, you were pretending you were Marla Graim, the feelies star, and him Sidney Harch meeting you in the bar to give you a spy capsule.

It was all my father's fault. Imagine him getting angry because I wouldn't take a job burning brush. What kind of work is that for an 18-year-old girl anyway? I know my folks were hard pressed for money but that was no excuse for the way he shouted at me.

We had the fight over lunch but it was after six o'clock before I got the chance to sneak out of the house. I went down to the Tavern because I knew the old man would be madder than a tele in a lead barrel when he found out. There was no way I could keep it from him, of course. He questioned me every time I came home.

The Tavern is a crossroads place where the talent gets together to compare notes, and talk about jobs. I'd only been in there once before, and that time with my father. He warned me not to go there alone because a lot of the jags used the place. You could smell the stuff all over the main room. There was pink smoke from a hyro bowl drifting up around the rafters. Someone had a Venusian Oin filter going. There was a lot of talent there for so early in the evening.

I found an empty corner of the bar and ordered a blue fire because I'd seen Marla Graim ask for one in the feelies. The barman stared at me sharply and I suspected he was a tele, but he didn't pry. After a while he floated my drink up to me and 'ported away the money. I sipped the drink the way I'd seen Marla Graim do, but it was too sweet. I tried not to let my face show anything.

The bar mirror gave me a good view of the room and I kept looking into it as though I was expecting somebody. Then this big blond young man came through the front door. I saw him in the mirror and immediately knew he was going to take the seat beside me. I'm not exactly a prescient, but sometimes those things are obvious.

He came across the room, moving with a gladiator ease between the packed tables. That's when I pretended I was Marla Graim waiting at a Port Said bar to pick up a spy capsule from Sidney Harch like in the feelie I'd seen on Sunday.

This fellow did look a little like Harch – curly hair, dark blue eyes, face all sharp angles as if it had been chiselled by a sculptor who'd left the job uncompleted.

He took the stool beside me as I'd known he would, and ordered a blue fire, easy on the sugar. Naturally, I thought this was a get-acquainted gambit and wondered what to say to him. Suddenly, it struck me as an exciting idea to just ride along with the Marla Graim plot until it came time to leave.

He couldn't do anything to stop me even if he was a 'porter. You see, I'm a pyro and that's a good enough defence for anyone. I glanced down at my circa-twenty skirt and shifted until the slit exposed my garter the way I'd seen Marla Graim do it. This blond lad didn't give it a tumble. He finished his drink, and ordered another.

I whiffed him for one of the cokes, but he was dry. No jag. The other stuff in the room was getting through to me, though, and I was feeling dizzy. I knew I'd have to leave soon and I'd never get another chance to be a Marla Graim type; so I said, "What's yours?"

Oh, he knew I was talking to him all right, but he didn't even look up. It made me mad. A girl has some pride and there I'd unbent enough to start the conversation! There was an ashtray piled with scraps of paper in front of him. I concentrated on it and the paper suddenly flamed. I'm a good pyro when I want to be. Some men have been kind enough to say I could start a fire without the talent. But with a prying father like mine how could I ever know?

The fire got this fellow's attention. He knew I'd started it. He just glanced at me once and turned away.

"Leave me alone," he said. "I'm a *Nothing*."

* * *

I don't know what it was. Maybe I have a little of the tele like that doctor said once, but I knew he was telling the truth. It wasn't one of those gags like you see in the feelies. You know – where there are two comedians and one says, "What's yours?" And the other one answers, "Nothing." Only all the time he's levitating the other guy's chair and juggling half a dozen things behind his back, no hands.

You know the gag. It's been run into the ground. Well, when he said that, it kind of set me back. I'd never seen a real-life *Nothing* before. Oh, I knew there were some. In the government preserves and such, but I'd never been like this – right next to one.

"Sorry," I said. "I'm a pyro."

He glanced at the ashes in the tray and said, "Yeah, I know."

"There's not much work for pyros any more," I said. "It's the only talent I have." I turned and looked at him. Handsome in spite of being a *Nothing*. "What did you do?" I asked.

"I ran away," he said. "I'm a fugitive from the Sonoma Preserve."

That made my blood tingle. Not only a *Nothing*, but a fugitive, too. Just like in the feelies. I said, "Do you want to hide out at my place?"

That brought him around. He looked me over and he actually

blushed. Actually! I'd never seen a man blush before. That fellow certainly was loaded with firsts for me.

"People might get the wrong idea when I'm caught," he said. "I'm sure to be caught eventually. I always am."

I was really getting a feeling for that woman-of-the-world part. "Why not enjoy your freedom then?" I asked.

I let him see a little more through the circa-twenty slit. He actually turned away! Imagine.

That's when the police came. They didn't make any fuss. I'd noticed these two men standing just inside the door watching us. Only I'd thought they were watching me. They came across the room and one of them bent over this fellow.

"All right, Claude," he said. "Come quietly."

The other took my arm and said, "You'll have to come, too, sister."

I jerked away from him. "I'm not your sister," I said.

"Oh, leave her alone, fellows," said Claude. "I didn't tell her anything. She was just trying to pick me up."

"Sorry," said the cop. "She comes, too."

That's when I began to get scared. "Look," I said. "I don't know what this is all about."

The man showed me the snout of a hypo gun in his pocket. "Stop the commotion and come quietly, sister, or I'll have to use this," he said.

So who wants to go to sleep? I went quietly, praying we'd run into my father or someone I knew so I could explain things. But no such luck.

The police had a plain old jet buggy outside with people clustered around looking at it. A 'porter in the crowd was having fun jiggling the rear end up and down off the ground. He was standing back with his hands in his pockets, grinning.

The cop who'd done all the talking just looked towards this 'porter and

FRANK HERBERT

A giant amongst science fiction writers. Frank Herbert's novel of life on the desert planet Arrakis, *Dune*, quickly attained cult status winning both Nebula and Hugo awards and bringing him to a wider audience outside the field. He soon produced two sequels.

Many of his novels since his first, *Dragon in the Sea,* have been vivid psychological dramas, the adventure supplementing the conflict between the major characters. *Dragon in the Sea* (or *Under Pressure* as it was originally titled in America) deals with the effects of stress on the crew of a submarine of the future. *The Green Brain* is a novel of an ecological disaster befalling the earth through man's thoughtlessness and which may be rectified by co-operation with its mutated insects.

Herbert is reputed to have been paid the largest ever advance for a science fiction book (over £500,000) for the fourth novel in the *Dune* series, *The God-Emperor of Dune.*

***The Nothing* takes as its subject the damage that generations of random marriages can do to a population of mutants.**

the fellow lost his grin and hurried away. I knew then the cop was a tele, although he hadn't touched my mind. They're awfully sensitive about their code of ethics, some of those teles.

It was fun riding in that old jet buggy. I'd never been in one before. One of the cops got in back with Claude and me. The other one drove. It was the strangest feeling, flying up over the bay on the tractors. Usually, whenever I wanted to go someplace, I'd just ask, polite like, was there a 'porter around and then I'd think of where I wanted to go and the 'porter would set me down there quick as a wink.

Of course, I wound up in some old gent's apartment now and then. Some 'porters do that sort of thing for a fee. But a pyro doesn't have to worry about would-be Casanovas. No old gent is going to fool around when his clothes are on fire.

Well, the jet buggy finally set down in the old hospital grounds way back up in the sticks and the cops took us to the main building and into a little office. Walking, mind you. It was shady in the office – not enough lights – and it took a minute for my eyes to adjust after the bright lights in the hall. When they did adjust and I saw the old codger behind the desk I did a real double take. It was Mensor Williams. Yeah. The *Big All*. Anything anybody else can do he can do better.

Somebody threw a switch somewhere and the lights brightened. "Good evening, Miss Carlysle," he said and his little goatee bobbled.

Before I could make a crack about ethics against reading minds, he said, "I'm not intruding into your mental processes. I've merely scanned forward to a point where I learn your name."

A prescient, too!

"There really wasn't any need to bring her," he told the cops. "But it was inevitable that you would." Then he did the funniest thing. He turned to Claude and nodded his head towards me. "How do you like her, Claude?" he asked. Just like I was something offered for sale or something!

Claude said, "Is she the one, Dad?"

Dad! That one rocked me. The *Big All* has a kid and the kid's a *Nothing*!

"She's the one," said Williams.

Claude kind of squared his shoulders and said, "Well, I'm going to throw a stick into the works. I won't do it!"

"Yes, you will," said Williams.

This was all way over my head and I'd had about enough anyway. I said, "Now wait a minute, gentlemen, or I'll set the place on fire! I mean literally!"

"She can do it, too," said Claude, grinning at his father.

"But she won't," said Williams.

"Oh, won't I?" I said. "Well, you just try and stop me!"

"No need to do that," said Williams. "I've seen what's going to happen."

Just like that! These prescients give me the creeps. Sometimes I wonder if they don't give themselves the creeps. Living for them must be like repeating a part you already know. Not for me. I said. "What would happen if I did something different from what you'd seen?"

Williams leaned forward with an interested look in his eyes. "It's never happened," he said. "If it did happen once, that'd be a real precedent."

I can't be sure, but looking at him there, I got the idea he'd really be interested to see something happen different from his forecast. I thought of starting a little fire, maybe in the papers on his desk. But somehow the idea didn't appeal to me. It wasn't that any presence was in my mind telling me not to. I don't know exactly what it was. I just didn't *want* to do it. I said, "What's the meaning of all this double talk?"

The old man leaned back and I swear he seemed kind of disappointed.

He said, "It's just that you and Claude are going to be married."

I opened my mouth to speak and nothing came out. Finally, I managed to stammer. "You mean you've looked into the future and seen us *married*? How many kids we're going to have and everything like that?"

"Well, not everything," he said. "All things in the future aren't clear to us. Only certain main-line developments. And we can't see too far into the future for most things. The past is easier. That's been fixed immovably."

"And what if we don't want to?" asked Claude.

"Yeah," I said. "What about that?" But I have to admit the idea wasn't totally repulsive. As I've said, Claude looked like Sidney Harch, only younger. He had something – you can call it animal magnetism if you wish.

The old man just smiled. "Miss Carlysle," he said, "do you honestly object to . . .?"

"As long as I'm going to be in the family you can call me Jean," I said.

I was beginning to feel fatalistic about the whole thing. My Great Aunt Harriet was a prescient and I'd had experience with them. Now I was remembering the time she told me my kitty was going to die and I hid it in the old cistern and that night it rained and filled the cistern. Naturally the kitty drowned. I never forgave her for not telling me how the kitty was going to die.

Old Williams looked at me and said, "At least *you're* being reasonable."

"I'm not," said Claude.

So I told them about my Great Aunt Harriet.

"It's the nature of things," said Williams. "Why can't you be as reasonable as she's being, son?"

Claude just sat there with the original stone face.

"Am I so repulsive?" I asked.

He looked at me then. Really looked. I tell you I got warm under it. I know I'm not repulsive. Finally, I guess I blushed.

"You're not repulsive," he said. "I just object to having my whole life set out for me like a chess match."

Stalemate. We sat there for a minute or so, completely silent. Presently Williams turned to me and said, "Well, Miss Carlysle, I presume you're curious about what's going on here."

"I'm not a moron," I said. "This is one of the *Nothing* Preserves."

"Correct," he said. "Only it's more than that. Your education includes the knowledge of how our talents developed from radiation mutants. Does it also include the knowledge of what happens to extremes from the norm?"

Every schoolkid knows that, of course. So I told him. Sure I knew that the direction of development was towards the average. That genius parents tend to have children less smart than they are. This is just general information.

Then the old man threw me the twister. "The talents are disappearing, my dear," he said.

I just sat there and thought about that for a while. Certainly I knew it'd been harder lately to get a 'porter, even one of the "old gent" kind.

"Each generation has more children without talents or with talents greatly dulled," said Williams. "We will never reach a point where there are absolutely none, but what few remain will be needed for special jobs in the public interest."

"You mean if I have kids they're liable to be *Nothings*?" I asked.

"Look at your own family," he said. "Your great aunt was a prescient. Have there been any others in your family?"

"Well, no, but . . ."

"The prescient talent is an extreme," he said. "There are fewer than 1,000 left. There are nine of us in my category. I believe you refer to us as the *Big All*."

"But we've got to do something!" I said. "The world'll just go to pot!"

"We *are* doing something," he said. "Right here and on eight other preserves scattered around the world. We're reviving the mechanical and tool skills which supported the pre-talent civilisation and we're storing the instruments which will make a rebirth of that civilisation possible."

He raised a warning hand. "But we must move in secrecy. The world's not yet ready for this information. It would cause a most terrible panic if this were to become known."

"Well, you're prescient. What does happen?" I asked him.

"Unfortunately, none of us are able to determine that," he said. "Either it's an unfixed line or there's some interference which we can't surmount." He shook his head and the goatee wiggled. "There's a cloudy area in the near future beyond which we can't see. None of us."

That scared me. A prescient may give you the creeps, but it's nice to know there's a future into which someone can see. It was as if there suddenly wasn't any future at all! I began to cry a little.

"And our children will be *Nothings*," I said.

"Well, not exactly," said Williams. "Some of them, maybe, but we've taken the trouble of comparing your gene lines – yours and Claude's. You've a good chance of having offspring who will be prescient or telepathic or both. A better than 70 per cent chance." His voice got pleading. "The world's going to need that chance."

Claude came over and put a hand on my shoulder. It sent a delicious tingle up my spine. Suddenly, I got a little flash of his thoughts – a picture of us kissing. I'm not really a tele, but like I said, sometimes I get glimmers.

Claude said, "Okay. I guess there's no sense fighting the inevitable. We'll get married."

No more argument. We all traipsed into another room and there was a preacher with everything ready for us, even the ring. Another prescient. He'd come more than 100 miles to perform the ceremony, he said.

*   *   *

Afterwards, I let Claude kiss me once. I was having trouble realising that I was married. Mrs. Claude Williams. But that's the way it is with the inevitable, I guess.

The old man took my arm then and said there was one small precaution. I'd be going off the grounds from time to time and there'd always be the chance of some unethical tele picking my brains.

They put me under an anesthetube and when I came out of it I had a silver grid in my skull. It itched some, but they said that it would go away. I'd heard of this thing. They called it a blanket.

Mensor Williams said, "Now go home and get your things. You won't need to tell your parents any more than that you have a government job. Come back as soon as you're able."

"Get me a 'porter," I said.

"The grounds are gridded against teleporters," he said. "I'll have to send you in a jet buggy."

And so he did.

I was home in 10 minutes.

I went up the stairs to my house. It was after nine by then. My father was waiting inside the door.

"A fine time for an 18-year-old girl to be coming home!" he shouted and he made a tele stab at my mind to see what I'd been up to. These teles and their ethics! Well, he ran smack dab into the blanket and maybe you think that didn't set him back on his heels. He got all quiet suddenly.

I said, "I have a government job. I just came back for my things." Time enough to tell them about the marriage later. They'd have kicked up a fine rumpus if I'd said anything then.

Mama came in and said, "My little baby with a government job! How much does it pay?"

I said, "Let's not be vulgar."

Papa sided with me. "Of course not, Hazel," he said. "Leave the kid alone. A government job! What do you know! Those things pay plenty. Where is it, baby?"

I could see him wondering how much he could tap me for to pay his bills and I began to wonder if I'd have any money at all to keep up the pretence. I said, "The job's at Sonoma Preserve."

Papa said, "What do they need with a pyro up there?"

I got a brilliant inspiration. I said, "To keep the *Nothings* in line. A little burn here, a little burn there. You know."

That struck my father as funny. When he could stop laughing he said, "I know you, honey. I've watched your think tank pretty close. You'll take care of yourself and no funny business. Do they have nice safe quarters for you up there?"

"The safest," I said.

I felt him take another prod at my blanket and withdraw. "Government work is top secret," I said.

"Sure. I understand," he said.

So I went to my room and got my things packed. The folks made some more fuss about my going away so suddenly, but they cooled down when I told them I had to go at once or lose the chance at the job.

Papa finally said, "Well, if the government isn't safe, then nothing is."

They kissed me good-bye and I promised to write and to visit home on my first free weekend. "Don't worry, Papa," I said.

The jet buggy took me back to the preserve. When I went into the office, Claude, my husband, was sitting across the desk from his father.

The old man had his hand to his forehead and there were beads of perspiration showing where the fingers didn't cover. Presently, he lowered his hands and shook his head.

"Well?" asked Claude.

"Not a thing," said the old man.

I moved a little bit into the room but they didn't notice me.

"Tell me the truth, Dad," said Claude. "How far ahead did you see us?"

Old Mensor Williams lowered his head and sighed. "All right, son," he said. "You deserve the truth. I saw you meet Miss Carlysle at the Tavern and not another thing. We had to trace her by old-fashioned methods and compare your gene lines like I said. The rest is truth. You know I wouldn't lie to you."

I cleared my throat and they both looked at me. Claude jumped up out of his chair and faced me. "We can get an annulment," he said. "No one has the right to play with other peoples' lives like that."

He looked so sweet and little-boy-like standing there. I knew suddenly I didn't want an annulment. I said, "The younger generation has to accept its responsibilities sometime."

Mensor Williams got an eager look in his eyes. I turned to the old man and said, "Was that 70 per cent figure correct?"

"Absolutely correct, my dear," he said. "We've checked every marriageable female he's met because he carries my family's dominant line. Your combination was the best. Far higher than we'd hoped for."

"Is there anything else you can tell us about our future?" I asked.

He shook his head. "It's all cloudy," he said. "You're on your own."

I got that creepy feeling again and looked up at my husband. Little laugh wrinkles creased at the corners of Claude's eyes and he smiled. Then another thought struck me. If we were on our own, that meant we were shaping our own future. It wasn't fixed. And no nosy prescient could come prying in on us, either. A woman kind of likes that idea. Especially on her wedding night.

Mix-up

BY GEORGE COLLYN

POINT ONE: and before I say one word more . . .

. . . That is, before the Federal Transport Authority slaps down a restraint injunction on the grounds of libel.

Let me say right here and now that the fault which created the troubles listed below has by now been completely eradicated and there is no possibility of its future recurrence. Therefore use your local teleportation unit without fear. It is 99 per cent safe.

*   *   *

Second point: Have you the faintest inkling as to the workings of the teleportation system?

Of course you haven't. Since when has man not taken for granted the technological advances presented for his convenience? After all, did the railway passenger of the 19th-century comprehend the marvels of steam locomotion? Or had the 20th-century air-line traveller the remotest notion as to the principle of the jet engine?

No – to them all that mattered was that they were transported from place to place with a minimum of inconvenience. And the same goes for you today as you are whisked from cubicle to cubicle over the teleportation system. So let's get some idea into your minds as to the principle of the thing before we go any one step further.

All material objects, when they are analysed down to their lowest common denominator below the level of their atomic structure, are made of the same basic "stuff" – to keep this simple let us call it matter. Matter forms the building bricks out of which, dependent upon the molecular arrangement, all things, be they a T-bone steak or a pint of sea-water, are made up.

Since the time at the beginning of the present century when man discovered the means to analyse, reduce and reconstruct this matter, the power of technology to alleviate material shortage has been considerably strengthened.

Take the Moira. No good home would be without one but now many people know that Moira is not just a pretty name but stands for Matter, Organic and Inorganic Reconstruction Apparatus? Let us just remember our operational procedure. You take the key code for whatever it is you require – say a new shirt. You slip it into the slot

42

provided and fill the hopper with the raw material – a couple of pints of sea-water, a pound or two of sand or, for that matter, an old shirt.

The Moira breaks down the sea-water or whatever it is and thus provided with its basic material, reconstructs the atomic structure in the way indicated by the code-key; which in this instance happens to be for a Gay-Glo "Glam-man" shirt – "expressly tailored for YOU in Gay-Glo's own laboratory".

You knew that you say?

In that case you have grasped the fundamentals of teleportation because, after all, physically a man is no more and no less than any other material compound – just a bit more complicated.

When you step into a transmission booth and dial your arrival number the transmission unit analyses your make-up and at the same time – alarming as it sounds – physically disintegrates you into basic matter. At the identical moment the memory banks transmit the information regarding your composition to the reception unit where you are put together again from the detritus of some previous traveller, eked out if necessary from the unit's matter-hopper.

It sounds alarming I know but in effect it is little different from the biological process; since what after all are the genetic chromosomes but computer programs? There is always the fear that once disintegrated, always disintegrated, but the process is virtually instantaneous. It isn't of course since it all takes place at the speed of light but, since light goes round the world seven times in a second, I defy any living man to distinguish between that and instantaneity.

Still it's strange to think how many people there are walking around today who started out in life as a couple of gallons of Atlantic. Never mind, there's nothing to be alarmed about. Hardly anything can go wrong.

But . . .

* * *

The obvious trouble with teleportation is that it utilises tight-beam radio waves and however tight the beam and no matter how perfect there always exists a risk that it may be subject to interference. How often for example have you sat with your video set slightly out of tune so that although you are getting C.B.S. New York loud and clear on channel 748 you are also picking up a faint image of B.B.C. International on channel 147?

One July day just three years ago, in the early afternoon E.S.T., or should we say early evening G.M.T. (rapid transatlantic travel can be very upsetting timewise) a minute, indeed infinitesimal part in the equipment of Teleportation Unit NYTS27815 (U.S.) in Times Square, New York City, went very slightly on the blink. It was a very small part and it was a very small fault but it meant that there was a limited amount of interference between channel 27J815 and 27K815.

Interference which began at a quarter past noon E.S.T. and continued intermittently; since it only occurred when both channels were in use and beamed simultaneously to the same destination; until three minutes before three when the condition became critical and automatic correction took place.

In that time a young salesman from Poughskeepie found on arrival in Sunset Unit, Los Angeles that he was holding a bag containing 350,000 dollar/sterling interchange credits while Alan B. Schumaker, a courier for the Chase Manhattan Bank standing in an adjacent cubicle, was left holding a bag of sample Moira baby-products code keys which represented five fragrances of talcum powder, two brands of disposable nappies and a portable crib. While a 30-year-old gerontologist called Spivak, en route from New York to the French Riviera, lost in transit the baby-blue eyes with which he had been born and somehow acquired the green-flecked-with-gold irises which had previously been the chief stock-in-trade of a gigolo by the name of Carlos who was returning from a most unpleasant time with a senile Daughter of the American Revolution to the compartive calm of the Promenade des Anglais.

Despite these minor upsets in the lives of four erstwhile carefree people, the mistakes till then had been of relatively little importance. However, at 2.51 E.S.T. Professor Irwin J. (for Joe) Black, lecturer in 20th-century literature at Columbia University, 35, sun-tanned, dark and handsome; and Miss Dorothy Simone, slim, ethereally blonde and indescribably beautiful 26-year-old video star; the former alone, the latter surrounded by ecstatic fans; entered respectively booths 41 and 71 of the Times Square Unit.

At 2.52 finger for finger in time they both dialled LO52781 (U.K.). One-tenth of a second later the tall dark man and the slim fair lady arrived in booths 28 and 42 of the Berkeley Square Unit in London.

* * *

Dorothy swept out of her booth with the imperious nonchalance born of a dozen temperamental and artistic tantrums but noticed nothing untoward save the shameful effrontery of several members of the public who disgracefully ignored her presence. Still with imperial majesty she swept along the Turkish-carpeted and gilt-mirrored corridors of that showplace of Teleportation Units. Less vain than acutely aware of her own stunning beauty she felt her temper rise almost to boiling point as a very handsome young man with a brown suit, brown hair and browned skin approached her showing neither any sign of recognition nor, what was worse still, any flicker of admiration.

Dorothy was in her way a connoisseur of masculine beauty but this time her aesthetic appreciation was marred by the slight to her pride. Walking to stand in the way of this presumptuous young man she would have spoken if she had not been brought up short physically and mentally by the realisation that the corridor turned sharp right at that point and what she had been walking towards in the past few minutes had been no young man but an image in a mirror.

Irwin had reality thrust upon him with much greater speed. This was partly due to the fact that he was not accustomed to step from a TP booth into the face of a screaming mob of fans and Press. More so it was because his brain issued walking instructions calculated to move feet shod in rather large suede brogues; which instructions were received by legs terminating in flimsy constructions made of a few square inches of leather, a strap and three-inch high stiletto heels.

To the immense titillated delight of a thousand males and pressmen the body of a delicate but well-constructed video star, albeit with the brain of an English professor, went headlong to the floor.

Their reactions were mutually out-of-character with their outward form. Travellers utilising the first-floor booths of the Berkeley Square TP Unit were treated to the sight of a six-foot, athletically built and fully adult male indulging in a fit of hysterics; while half the male population of Greater London watched entranced the rosebud-shaped and rose petal-tinted lips of an angelic blonde giving forth with language which would not have disgraced an argument between a Billingsgate porter and a bargee.

* * *

Dorothy was distinctly uncomfortable. Something was wrong but she did not know what it was. For all she knew it was something peculiarly masculine. As it happens it was simply that as a non-smoker she failed to recognise the withdrawal symptoms of nicotine starvation in the body of an ardent 30-a-day man. Plagued with incomprehensible pangs she took little part in the conversation that was proceeding. Cool, calm and composed she sat, and inwardly seethed.

Irwin, on the other hand, overwhelmed, looked a perfect picture of innocent and helpless appeal. His blond hair in disarray, attractive disarray of course; his full gentian violet eyes rendered more glisteningly startling by being full of tears; the lower lip trembling in dismay – the appeal of Dorothy Simone as one of the world's most beautiful women had always rested on the paternal-lover instinct men have in response to helplessness.

Now to David Wallace, representative in England of Teleportation (U.S.) Inc, facing the vision of loveliness across his desk, there came the irresistible urge to take her . . . him . . . er . . . Irwin into his arms and kiss away those tears. The only thing that held him back was the thought that he and Irv Black had grown up on the same block, had played together, gone to High School together, roistered round college in partnership and these things built up a constraint. It was all rather confusing and altogether rather unfair.

"But Dave," pleaded Irwin, "it's all very well saying how sorry you are but what are you going to do about it?"

"Now don't you worry Miss Si- I mean Irv. I assure you Teleportation Inc will pay you a very adequate compensation for this unfortunate accident."

"What good is compensation? I want my body back. What sort of fool do you think I'll look to my students like this?"

"I'm sure you look very nice. Don't you think you could perhaps reconcile yourself. After all, you're a very attractive woman now. I'm sure there are millions of schoolgirls all over the world who could ask for nothing better than to grow up looking like that."

"You forget that I never was a schoolgirl and I've never had any ambition to grow into anything but a perfectly normal masculine male. And now all I want is to be back in that body there and if Miss Simone can bear to give it up I'm sure she'd like nothing better than to be back in here where she belongs."

"Well it's all a bit difficult but immediately we heard about your accident we put our research team to work and there's every hope they'll come up with some sort of an answer in a couple of months or so. They've never failed us yet."

"A couple of months he says. What am I to do in the meantime? I'm due to lecture at University College tomorrow. How do you think the students will feel about a world famous dumb blonde lecturing them on Logical Positivism in Twentieth-Century Science Fiction?

"Please don't forget me," broke in Dorothy, her new bass vocal chords not yet fully under control, "I'm supposed to be acting tomorrow in a play that's going out over an international hook-up that could be the turning point of my career. A fine sight I shall look now playing an 18-year-old girl."

"All I can suggest," said David, "is that you attempt, just for the one day, to fulfil each other's commitments. We'll give you every help we can of course. For a start I think we'd better get you both rooms at the TP Unit Berkeley Hotel so that you can talk things over."

"A double room," said Dorothy, with resignation but firmness.

"Certainly not," shouted Irwin, "I'm not sharing any room with that . . . that . . . man!" Always a hypochondriac, Irwin had contemplated every accident or sickness that flesh is heir to but there was one

GEORGE COLLYN

Is 43 and lives in South-West Lancashire. Unmarried, he currently works in education as a senior teacher in a large comprehensive school and as an examination administrator with the regional CSE Examination Board. He began writing in the 1960's as an antidote to the loneliness of hotel bedrooms and has had stories and articles published in a wide variety of newspapers and magazines. He edits a philatelic magazine.

***Mix-up* was his first published story and began a happy association between the author and *New Worlds* magazine, forming part of the so-called "new wave" revival of science-fiction writing in Britain in the late sixties. The idea for this story was "quite blatantly filched" from a novel by Thorne Smith as he readily admits.**

thing from which he had considered himself immune. Paternity he did not mind but what red-blooded male wants to run the risk of maternity?

"Certainly a double room," insisted Dorothy. "Whatever you may think of them, that face and that body are my chief assets. I'm not leaving that man alone with them to deal with them as he sees fit."

"But," stammered Irwin.

"Are you bashful?" asked Dorothy. "Look at it this way. You've spent your life with this body and I've spent mine with that. We should know what one another looks like in the raw. Who can afford modesty at a time like this?"

But Irwin was in tears again.

* * *

The next morning it took Dorothy two hours to get Irwin dressed and ready. Of course he had to try to dress himself in which attempt he succeded only after a long diatribe against the ridiculous impracticality of feminine undergarments. Then he had to do it over again after a lengthy protest from Dorothy as to his complete lack of dress-sense and colour consciousness. Finally came the attempt to make make up his face which resulted in three abortive mockeries before Dorothy was able to pronounce him fit to be seen by the world.

At last the mixed-up couple made their way to the first of their appointments. Teleportation Inc had provided a miniaturised transmitter and receiver, the former hidden in a pearl necklace and around Irwin's throat the latter concealed in Dorothy's ear. So Irwin, hastily introduced as an old and valued friend, was able to prompt Dorothy on the names of the welcoming dignitaries and also to feed her the lecture sentence by sentence for delivery to the audience.

It was a wow.

Always fairly shy in public, nobody faulted Irwin for his knowledge, only for his style of speaking which was hurried, dull and uninspiring. For the first time his material was delivered with all the skill of a born actress and she made it live. The result was that the lecture was applauded by a standing ovation. Now Dorothy was a video actress who had never known a live audience and the experience went to her head. She bowed and waved at the applauding throng.

As it were in thanks for the experience she turned and kissed Irwin which action of course sent the audience into fresh frenzies. It was a sensation.

Six hours and a rehearsal later the transmitter was tucked into one of Irwin's ties and round Dorothy's neck and the receiver was hidden under carefully arranged fair hair. Irwin was making the debut of his acting career. Luckily the play was a good old-fashioned weepie in which he had to take the part of a schmaltz-ridden deaf and dumb girl. All he had to do was to move according to Dorothy's instructions and register shock, horror and dismay which, faced with a battery of lights and video cameras, called for no acting ability whatsoever.

The only awkward moment came at the climax when the hero had to take him in his arms. Every masculine instinct told him to haul off and poke this fellow in the nose but it so happened that, though the brain patterns were masculine, the nervous and glandular systems were still 100 per cent feminine and a wave of pleasured feminine id overcame the repelled masculine ego, and he managed to respond automatically with perfect correctness.

* * *

. . . "Dot baby." This was Abe Schultz, Miss Simone's agent, calling her from Hollywood. "Dotty, honey, you were ab-so-lutely great. Al and I sat here and watched your performance and baby there wasn't a dry eye between the two of us. Strictly between ourselves, honey, we've been kinda worried about you lately. We were getting the idea you were losing that good old cuddlesome image – getting kinda independent if you know what I mean.

But tonight I take it all back: you were just great and everyone, but everyone, thinks so too. The offers are flowing in and I've a beaut lined up for you. It's a remake of an old movie called *Turnabout* by a fellow called Thorne Smith and it's about how this guy and his wife get swapped round because they got in bad with a magic statue. Now I know you're the last one I can think of to make like a man but if it comes off you're made, 'cos it could be good, and the money's even better. Think you could handle it?"

* * *

"Black," said Dean Lockweiler, on the visiphone from New York, "the faculty and I felt we should phone you to record our appreciation of the reports reaching us of the reception accorded your lecture in London. I must confess there has been a certain amount of criticism expressed of late as to the suitablility of your position here as a leading authority in the field of English Literature.

"The general feeling rightly or wrongly was that, although pure cerebration might be permissible, indeed necessary, in the earlier patterns of university life, today, when so much of our output has been devoted to the growing channels of mass communication, there is a need for the public expression of one's knowledge to be fully recognised.

"Up to this time, as I say, we felt this faculty was lacking in yourself but following your success of yesterday I can say with all fairness that we expect you to rise to great heights in the career we are now planning for you."

* * *

"Well," said Dave Wallace, "I can't say how sorry we are that this has taken so long but you will appreciate that there have been serious technical problems to overcome and in fact we feel that in relation to that difficulty six months is a very short time indeed. Anyway that's enough of the apologies, I'm sure you're much more interested in what we've worked out for you."

He paused to see how his audience were taking it. He had to admit that he was more than a little disappointed and puzzled. Despite their previous insistent demands that the firm's mistake be rectified they seemed to be taking the news of that impending rectification with a startling indifference. Also, for a couple so antagonistic towards one another when last he saw them, they seemed remarkably friendly. He continued.

"It would seem that interference between two parallel beams during teleportation caused your two brains to be transposed without otherwise physically affecting you. Now although we cannot repeat the operation with any certainty of success we have adapted a teleportation unit to withdraw and transpose your respective memory banks – in other words to transfer that sum of experience which create your personalities and awareness from one body to the other." He smiled triumphantly at them.

Dorothy-ex-Irwin smiled shyly back. "I'm honestly terribly sorry you have had all this trouble for nothing but you see I think that after all it won't be necessary," she/he paused and glanced at her/his partner. "Irwin and I have found out how very much more content we are today. Both of us were successful in our careers but complete failures in our personal lives and that failure was beginning to affect our work. It almost seems that the accident was meant to make better, more efficient and more successful people out of us. So you see we shan't be needing your machine after all."

"We can't anyway," broke in Irwin-ex-Dorothy, blushing very prettily "because last week I asked Dorothy to marry me and I'm very glad to say she accepted."

* * *

So that was a little over two years ago and despite the former Miss Simone's reputation for marriage-busting the partnership shows every sign of lasting and I see no reason why it should not continue to do so. After all, the one person we love above all others is ourself. What if we manage to externalise the self we grew up with and marry that self? If love can conquer all, think what ego-centred love can do.

Dorothy-ex-Irwin worked on for a time but abandoned her promising acting career in order to coach Irwin into becoming an equal authority on English Literature in which, since the former Miss Simone was always only artifically unintelligent, she was entirely successful – they are now the most powerful academic couple on the campus, in the whole of the 50 states of the Union for that matter.

Her departure from the public eye was hastened by the arrival of Irwin Junior, to be joined just a couple of months ago by Dorothy Junior – a fine pair of kids who are a credit to their parents. Most important of all, though, to them both is the work they are doing in advising those who find themselves in the same position as do the Blacks.

After all you can't expect a firm to spend six months and an awful lot of money in developing a complex apparatus and then leave it to rot. Therefore the Personality Transfer unit or PETER as it is known, has come into its own. There are plenty of brilliant and original minds entombed in bodies which are incurably sick or decaying in senility.

Equally there are healthy bodies supporting sick minds – the incurably but not psychically insane, the psychopaths, the condemned murderers of this world. What a service to mankind to transpose the two. On these occasions body and mind are sometimes compatible: more often however they are of different sexes, ages or races and it is to help these people in their adjustment that the Blacks are called in.

Also, and it is a little known fact, the PETER is now a regularly used device in the marriage guidance game. Let one partner have a fortnight's insight into the point of view of their husband or wife . . . Very good results have been achieved, but I can tell you, you can no longer be certain that your neighbour is the same person today as he was yesterday or will be tomorrow.

Time fuse

BY RANDALL GARRETT

COMMANDER BENEDICT kept his eyes on the rear plate as he activated the intercom. "All right, cut the power. We ought to be safe enough here."

As he released the intercom, Dr. Leicher, of the astronomical staff, stepped up to his side. "Perfectly safe," he nodded, "although even at this distance a star going nova ought to be quite a display."

Benedict didn't shift his gaze from the plate. "Do you have your instruments set up?"

"Not quite. But we have plenty of time. The light won't reach us for several hours yet. Remember, we were outracing it at 10 lights."

The commander finally turned, slowly letting his breath out in a soft sigh. "Dr. Leicher, I would say that this is just about the foulest coincidence that could happen to the first interstellar vessel ever to leave the Solar System."

Leicher shrugged. "In one way of thinking, yes. It is certainly true that we will never know, now, whether Alpha Centauri A ever had any planets. But, in another way, it is extremely fortunate that we should be so near a stellar explosion because of the wealth of scientific information we can obtain. As you say, it is a coincidence, and probably one that happens only once in a billion years. The chances of any particular star going nova are small. That we should be so close when it happens is of an extremely small order of probability."

RANDALL GARRETT

A regular contributor during the 1940's and '50's to the pulp magazines, especially *Analog* and *Astounding*.

Randall Phillips Garrett has produced work of varying quality and has often run foul of the critics. However, many agree that his *The Hunting Lodge* is his most brilliant work, a modern classic.

He has collaborated with such writers as Lin Carter, Avram Davidson and Robert Silverberg, producing with the latter many short stories, later incorporated into the novels *The Shrouded Planet* and *The Dawning Light*.

***Too Many Magicians* is a collection of many of his Lord D'arcy detective stories, originally published in *Analog*. Its central character, a police inspector lives in an alternate universe where magic is made possible under controlled conditions.**

***Time Fuse* finds Garrett considering a major disadvantage of a new form of interstellar travel making use of warped space-time while setting up who knows what kind of ripples in the fabric of our universe!**

Commander Benedict took off his cap and looked at the damp stain in the sweatband. "Nevertheless, Doctor, it is damned unnerving to come out of ultradrive a couple of hundred million miles from the first star ever visited by man and have to turn tail and run because the *damned* thing practically blows up in your face."

Leicher could see that Benedict was upset; he rarely used the same profanity twice in one sentence.

They had been downright lucky, at that. If Leicher hadn't seen the star begin to swell and brighten, if he hadn't known what it meant, or if Commander Benedict hadn't been quick enough in shifting the ship back into ultradrive – Leicher had a vision of an incandescent cloud of gaseous metal that had once been a spaceship.

The intercom buzzed. The commander answered, "Yes?"

"Sir, would you tell Dr. Leicher that we have everything set up now?"

Leicher nodded and turned to leave. "I guess we have nothing to do now but wait."

When the light from the nova did come, Commander Benedict was back at the plate again – the forward one, this time, since the ship had been turned around in order to align the astronomy lab in the nose with the star.

Alpha Centauri A began to brighten and spread. It made Benedict think of a light bulb connected through a rheostat, with someone turning that rheostat, turning it until the circuit was well overloaded.

The light began to hurt Benedict's eyes even at that distance and he had to cut down the receptivity in order to watch. After a while, he turned away from the plate. Not because the show was over, but simply because it had slowed to a point beyond which no change seemed to take place to the human eye.

Five weeks later, much to Leicher's chagrin, Commander Benedict announced that they had to leave the vicinity. The ship had only been provisioned to go to Alpha Centauri, scout the system without landing on any of the planets, and return. At 10 lights, top speed for the ultradrive, it would take better than three months to get back.

"I know you'd like to watch it go through the complete cycle," Benedict said, "but we can't go back home as a bunch of starved skeletons."

Leicher resigned himself to the necessity of leaving much of his work unfinished, and, although he knew it was a case of sour grapes, consoled himself with the thought that he could at least get most of the remaining information from the 500 in. telescope on Luna, four years from then.

As the ship slipped into the not-quite-space through which the ultradrive propelled it, Leicher began to consolidate the material he had already gathered.

* * *

Commander Benedict wrote in the log:

Fifty-four days out from Sol. Alpha Centauri has long since faced back into its pre-blowup state, since we have far outdistanced the light from its explosion. It now looks as it did two years ago. It . . .

"Pardon me, Commander," Leicher interrupted, "but I have something interesting to show you."

Benedict took his fingers off the keys and turned around in his chair, "What is it, Doctor?"

Leicher frowned at the papers in his hands. "I've been doing some work on the probability of that explosion happening just as it did, and I've come up with some rather frightening figures. As I said before, the probability was small. A little calculation has given us some information which makes it even smaller. For instance: with a possible error of plus or minus two seconds Alpha Centauri A began to explode the instant we came out of ultradrive!

"Now, the probability of that occurring comes out so small that it should happen only once in 10 to the 467 seconds."

It was Commander Benedict's turn to frown. "So?"

"Commander, the entire universe is only about 10 to the 17 seconds old. But to give you an idea, let's say that the chances of its happening are *once* in millions of trillions of years!"

Benedict blinked. The number, he realised, was totally beyond his comprehension – or anyone else's.

"Well, so what? Now it has happened that one time. That simply means that it will almost certainly never happen again!"

"True. But, Commander, when you back odds like that and win, the thing to do is look for some factor that is cheating in your favour. If you took a pair of dice and started throwing sevens, one right after another – for the next couple of thousand years – you'd begin to suspect they were loaded."

Benedict said nothing; he just waited expectantly.

"There is only one thing that could have done it. Our ship," Leicher said it quietly, without emphasis.

"What we know about the hyperspace, or superspace, or whatever it is we move through in ultradrive, is almost nothing. Coming out of it so near to a star might set up some sort of shock wave in normal space which would completely disrupt that star's internal balance, resulting in the liberation of unimaginably vast amounts of energy, causing that star to go nova.

"We can only assume that we ourselves were the fuse that set off that nova."

Benedict stood up slowly. When he spoke, his voice was a choking whisper. *"You mean the sun – Sol – might . . ."*

Leicher nodded. "I don't say that it definitely would. But the probability is that we were the cause of the destruction of Alpha Centauri A, and therefore might cause the destruction of Sol in the same way."

Benedict's voice was steady again. "That means that we cannot go back again, doesn't it? Even if we're not positive, we can't take the chance."

"Not necessarily. We can get fairly close before we cut out the drive,

and come in the rest of the way at sub-light speed. It'll take longer, and we'll have to go on half or one-third rations, but we *can* do it!"

"How far away?"

"I don't know what the minimum distance is, but I do know how we can gauge a distance. Remember, neither Alpha Centauri B or C were detonated. We'll have to cut our drive at least as far away from Sol as they are from A."

"I see." The Commander was silent for a moment, then: "Very well, Dr. Leicher. If that's the safest way, that's the only way."

Benedict issued the orders, while Leicher figured the exact point at which they must cut out the drive, and how long the trip would take. The rations would have to be cut down accordingly.

Commander Benedict's mind whirled around the monstrousness of the whole thing like some dizzy bee around a flower. What if there had been planets around Centauri A? What if they had been inhabited? Had he, albeit unwittingly, killed entire races of living, intelligent beings?

But, how could he have known? The drive had never been tested before. It couldn't be tested inside the Solar System – it was too fast. He and his crew had been volunteers, knowing that they might die when the drive went on.

Suddenly, Benedict gasped and slammed his fist down on the desk before him.

Leicher looked up. "What's the matter, Commander?"

"Suppose," came the answer, "just suppose that we have the same effect on a star when we *go into* ultradrive as we do when we come out of it?"

Leicher was silent for a moment, stunned by the possibility. There was nothing to say, anyway. They could only wait . . .

* * *

A little more than half a
light year from Sol, when the ship
reached the point where its occupants could see the
light that had left their home sun more than
seven months before, they watched it
become suddenly, horribly brighter.
A hundred thousand times brighter . . .

It's a good life

BY JEROME BIXBY

AUNT AMY WAS OUT ON THE FRONT PORCH, rocking back and forth in the high-backed chair and fanning herself, when Bill Soames rode his bicycle up the road and stopped in front of the house.

Perspiring under the afternoon "sun", Bill lifted the box of groceries out of the big basket over the front wheel of the bike, and came up the front path.

Little Anthony was sitting on the lawn, playing with a rat. He had caught the rat down in the basement – he had made it think that it smelled cheese, the most rich-smelling and crumbly-delicious cheese a rat had ever thought it smelled, and it had come out of its hole, and now Anthony had hold of it with his mind and was making it do tricks.

When the rat saw Bill Soames coming, it tried to run, but Anthony thought at it, and it turned a flip-flop on the grass, and lay trembling, its eyes gleaming in small black terror.

Bill Soames hurried past Anthony and reached the front steps, mumbling. He always mumbled when he came to the Fremont house, or passed by it, or even thought of it. Everybody did. They thought about silly things, things that didn't mean very much, like two-and-two-is-four-and-twice-is-eight and so on; they tried to jumble up their thoughts and keep them skipping back and forth, so Anthony couldn't read their minds. The mumbling helped. Because if Anthony got anything strong out of your thoughts, he might take a notion to do something about it – like curing your wife's sick headaches or your kid's mumps, or getting your old milk cow back on schedule, or fixing the privy. And while Anthony mightn't actually mean any harm, he couldn't be expected to have much notion of what was the right thing to do in such cases.

That was if he liked you. He might try to help you, in his way. And that could be pretty horrible.

If he didn't like you . . . well, that could be worse.

Bill Soames set the box of groceries on the porch railing, and stopped his mumbling long enough to say, "Everythin' you wanted, Miss Amy."

"Oh, fine, William," Amy Fremont said lightly. "My, ain't it terrible hot today?"

Bill Soames almost cringed. His eyes pleaded with her. He shook his head violently *no*, and then interrupted his mumbling again, though obviously he didn't want to: "Oh, don't say that, Miss Amy . . . it's fine, just fine. A real *good* day!"

Amy Fremont got up from the rocking chair, and came across the porch. She was a tall woman, thin, a smiling vacancy in her eyes. About a year ago, Anthony had got mad at her, because she'd told him he shouldn't have turned the cat into a cat-rug, and although he had always obeyed her more than anyone else, which was hardly at all, this time he'd snapped at her. With his mind. And that had been the end of Amy Fremont's bright eyes, and the end of Amy Fremont as everyone had known her. And that was when word got around in Peaksville (population: 46) that even the members of Anthony's own family weren't safe. After that, everyone was twice as careful.

Someday Anthony might undo what he'd done to Aunt Amy. Anthony's Mom and Pop hoped he would. When he was older, and maybe sorry. If it was possible, that is. Because Aunt Amy had changed a lot, and besides, now Anthony wouldn't obey anyone.

"Land alive, William," Aunt Amy said, "you don't have to mumble like that. Anthony wouldn't hurt you. My goodness, Anthony likes you!" She raised her voice and called to Anthony, who had tired of the rat and was making it eat itself. "Don't you, dear? Don't you like Mr. Soames?"

Anthony looked across the lawn at the grocery man – a bright, wet, purple gaze. He didn't say anything. Bill Soames tried to smile at him. After a second Anthony returned his attention to the rat. It had already devoured its tail, or at least chewed it off – for Anthony had made it bite faster than it could swallow, and little pink and red furry pieces lay around it on the green grass. Now the rat was having trouble reaching its hindquarters.

Mumbling silently, thinking of nothing in particular as hard as he could, Bill Soames went stiff-legged down the path, mounted his bicycle and pedalled off.

"We'll see you tonight, William," Aunt Amy called after him.

As Bill Soames pumped the pedals, he was wishing deep down that he could pump twice as fast, to get away from Anthony all the faster, and away from Aunt Amy, who sometimes just forgot how *careful* you had to be. And he shouldn't have thought that. Because Anthony caught it. He caught the desire to get away from the Fremont house as if it was something *bad*, and his purple gaze blinked, and he snapped a small, sulky thought after Bill Soames – just a small one, because he was in a good mood today, and besides, he liked Bill Soames, or at least didn't dislike him, at least today. Bill Soames wanted to go away – so, petulantly, Anthony helped him.

Pedalling with superhuman speed – or rather, appearing to, because in reality the bicycle was pedalling *him* – Bill Soames vanished down the road in a cloud of dust, his thin, terrified wail drifting back across the summer-like heat.

Anthony looked at the rat. It had devoured half its belly, and had died from pain. He thought it into a grave out deep in the cornfield – his father

had once said, smiling, that he might as well do that with the things he killed – and went around the house, casting his odd shadow in the hot, brassy light from above.

* * *

In the kitchen, Aunt Amy was unpacking the groceries. She put the goods on the shelves, and the meat and milk in the icebox, and the beet sugar and coarse flour in big cans under the sink. She put the cardboard box in the corner, by the door, for Mr. Soames to pick up next time he came. It was stained and battered and torn and worn fuzzy, but it was one of the few left in Peaksville. In faded red letters it said *Campbell's Soup*. The last cans of soup, or of anything else, had been eaten long ago, except for a small communal hoard which the villagers dipped into for special occasions – but the box lingered on, like a coffin, and when it and the other boxes were gone, the men would have to make some out of wood.

Aunt Amy went out the back, where Anthony's Mom – Aunt Amy's sister – sat in the shade of the house, shelling peas. The peas, every time Mom ran a finger along a pod, went *lollop-lollop-lollop* into the pan on her lap.

"William brought the groceries," Aunt Amy said. She sat down wearily in the straight-backed chair beside Mom, and began fanning herself again. She wasn't really old; but ever since Anthony had snapped at her with his mind, something had seemed to be wrong with her body as well as her mind, and she was tired all the time.

"Oh, good," said Mom. *Lollop* went the fat peas into the pan.

Everybody in Peaksville always said, "Oh, fine", or "Good", or "Say, that's swell!" when almost anything happened or was mentioned – even unhappy things like accidents or even deaths. They'd always say "Good", because if they didn't try to cover up how they really felt, Anthony might overhear with his mind, and then nobody knew what might happen. Like the time Mrs. Kent's husband, Sam, had come walking back from the graveyard, because Anthony liked Mrs. Kent and had heard her mourning.

Lollop.

"Tonight's television night," said Aunt Amy. "I'm glad. I look forward to it so much every week. I wonder what we'll see tonight?"

"Did Bill bring the meat?" asked Mom.

"Yes." Aunt Amy fanned herself, looking up at the featureless brassy glare of the sky. "Goodness, it's so hot! I wish Anthony would make it just a little cooler . . ."

"*Amy!*"

"Oh!" Mom's sharp tone had penetrated, where Bill Soames' agonised expression had failed. Aunt Amy put one thin hand to her mouth in exaggerated alarm. "Oh . . . I'm sorry, dear." Her pale blue eyes shuttled around, right and left, to see if Anthony was in sight. Not that it would make any difference if he was or wasn't – he didn't have to be near you to know what you were thinking. Usually, though, unless he had his attention on somebody, he would be occupied with thoughts of his own.

But some things attracted his attention – you could never be sure just what.

"This weather's just *fine*," Mom said.

Lollop.

"Oh, yes," Aunt Amy said. "It's a wonderful day. I wouldn't want it changed for the world!"

Lollop.

Lollop.

"What time is it?" Mom asked.

Aunt Amy was sitting where she could see through the kitchen window to the alarm clock on the shelf above the stove. "4.30," she said.

Lollop.

"I want tonight to be something special," Mom said. "Did Bill bring a good lean roast?"

"Good and lean, dear. They butchered just today, you know, and sent us over the best piece."

"Dan Hollis will be *so* surprised when he finds out that tonight's television party is a birthday party for him too!"

"Oh, I think he will! Are you sure nobody's told him?"

"Everybody swore they wouldn't."

"That'll be real nice," Aunt Amy nodded, looking off across the cornfield. "A birthday party."

"Well . . ." Mom put the pan of peas down beside her, stood up and brushed her apron. "I'd better get the roast on. Then we can set the table." She picked up the peas.

Anthony came around the corner of the house. He didn't look at them, but continued on down through the carefully kept garden – *all* the gardens in Peaksville were carefully kept, very carefully kept – and went past the rusting, useless hulk that had been the Fremont family car, and went smoothly over the fence and out into the cornfield.

"Isn't this a lovely day!" said Mom, a little loudly, as they went towards the back door.

Aunt Amy fanned herself. "A beautiful day, dear. Just *fine*!"

Out in the cornfield, Anthony walked between the tall rustling rows of green stalks. He liked to smell the corn. The alive corn overhead, and the old dead corn underfoot. Rich Ohio earth, thick with weeds and brown, dry-rotting ears of corn, passed between his bare toes with every step – he had made it rain last night so everything would smell and feel nice today.

He walked clear to the edge of the cornfield, and over to where a grove of shadowy green trees covered cool, moist, dark ground, and lots of leafy undergrowth, and jumbled moss-covered rocks, and a small spring that made a clear, clean pool.

Here Anthony liked to rest and watch the birds and insects and small animals that rustled and scampered and chirped about. He liked to lie on the cool ground and look up through the moving greenness overhead, and watch the insects flit in the hazy soft sunbeams that stood like slanting, glowing bars between ground and treetops. Somehow, he liked the thoughts of the little creatures in that place better than the thoughts outside; and while the thoughts he picked up here weren't very strong or very clear, he could get enough out of them to know what the little creatures liked and wanted, and he spent a lot of time making the grove more like what they wanted it to be.

The spring hadn't always been here; but one time he had found thirst in one small furry mind, and had brought subterranean water to the surface in a clear cold flow, and had watched blinking as the creature drank, feeling its pleasure. Later he had made the pool, when he found a small urge to swim.

He had made rocks and trees and bushes and caves, and sunlight here and shadows there, because he had felt in all the tiny minds around him the desire – or the instinctive want – for this kind of resting place, and that kind of mating place, and this kind of place to play, and that kind of home.

And somehow the creatures from all the fields and pastures around the grove seemed to know that this was a good place, for there were always more of them coming in – every time Anthony came out here there were more creatures than the last time, and more desires and needs to be tended to. Every time there would be some kind of creature he had never seen before, and he would find its mind, and see what it wanted, and then give it to it.

He liked to help them. He liked to feel their simple gratification.

Today, he rested beneath a thick elm, and lifted his purple gaze to a red and black bird that had just come to the grove. It twittered on a branch over his head, and hopped back and forth, and thought its tiny thoughts, and Anthony made a big, soft nest for it, and pretty soon it hopped in.

A long, brown, sleek-furred animal was drinking at the pool. Anthony found its mind next. The animal was thinking about a smaller creature that was scurrying along the ground on the other side of the pool, grubbing for insects. The little creature didn't know that it was in danger. The long, brown animal finished drinking and tensed its legs to leap, and Anthony thought it into a grave in the cornfield.

He didn't like those kinds of thoughts. They reminded him of the thoughts outside the grove. A long time ago some of the people outside had thought that way about *him*, and one night they'd hidden and waited for him to come back from the grove – and he'd just thought them all into the cornfield. Since then, the rest of the people hadn't thought that way – at least, very clearly. Now their thoughts were all mixed up and confusing whenever they thought about him or near him, so he didn't pay much attention.

He liked to help them too, sometimes – but it wasn't simple, or very gratifying either. They never thought happy thoughts when he did – just the jumble. So he spent more time out here.

He watched all the birds and insects and furry creatures for a while, and played with a bird, making it soar and dip and streak madly around tree trunks until, accidentally, when another bird caught his attention for a moment, he ran it into a rock. Petulantly, he thought the rock into a grave in the cornfield; but he couldn't do anything more with the bird. Not because it was dead, though it was; but because it had a broken wing. So he went back to the house. He didn't feel like walking back through the cornfield, so he just *went* to the house, right down into the basement.

It was nice down here. Nice and dark and damp and sort of fragrant, because once Mom had been making preserves in a rack along the far wall, and then she'd stopped coming down ever since Anthony had started spending time here, and the preserves had spoiled and leaked down and spread over the dirt floor, and Anthony liked the smell.

He caught another rat, making it smell cheese, and after he played with it, he thought it into a grave right beside the long animal he'd killed in the grove. Aunt Amy hated rats, and so he killed a lot of them, because he liked Aunt Amy most of all and sometimes did things that Aunt Amy wanted. Her mind was more like the little furry minds out in the grove. She hadn't thought anything bad at all about him for a long time.

After the rat, he played with a big black spider in the corner under the stairs, making it run back and forth until its web shook and shimmered in the light from the cellar window like a reflection in silvery water. Then he drove fruit flies into the web until the spider was frantic trying to wind them all up. The spider liked flies, and its thoughts were stronger than their's, so he did it. There was something bad in the way it liked flies, but it wasn't clear – and besides, Aunt Amy hated flies too.

He heard footsteps overhead – Mom moving around in the kitchen. He blinked his purple gaze, and almost decided to make her hold still – but instead he *went* up to the attic, and, after looking out of the circular window at the front end of the long V-roofed room for a while at the front lawn and the dusty road and Henderson's tip-waving wheatfield beyond, he curled into an unlikely shape and went partly to sleep.

Soon people would be coming for television, he heard Mom think.

He became more drowsy. He liked television night. Aunt Amy had always liked television a lot, so one time he had thought some for her, and a few other people had been there at the time, and Aunt Amy had felt disappointed when they wanted to leave. He'd done something to them for that – and now everybody came to television.

He liked all the attention he got when they did.

*   *   *

Anthony's father came home around 6.30, looking tired and dirty and bloody. He'd been over in Dunn's pasture with the other men, helping pick out the cow to be slaughtered this month and doing the job, and then butchering the meat and salting it away in Soame's icehouse. Not a job he cared for, but every man had his turn. Yesterday, he had helped scythe down old McIntyre's wheat. Tomorrow, they would start threshing. By hand. Everything in Peaksville had to be done by hand.

He kissed his wife on the cheek and sat down at the kitchen table. He smiled and said, "Where's Anthony?"

"Around someplace," Mom said.

Aunt Amy was over at the wood-burning stove, stirring the big pot of peas. Mom went back to the oven and opened it and basted the roast.

"Well, it's been a *good* day," Dad said. By rote. Then he looked at the mixing bowl and breadboard on the table. He sniffed at the dough. "M'm," he said. "I could eat a loaf all by myself, I'm so hungry."

"No one told Dan Hollis about its being a birthday party, did they?" his wife asked.

"Nope. We kept as quiet as mummies."

"We've fixed up such a lovely surprise!"

"Um? What?"

"Well . . . you know how much Dan likes music. Well, last week Thelma Dunn found a *record* in her attic!"

"No!"

"Yes! And we had Ethel sort of ask – you know, without really *asking* – if he had that one. And he said no. Isn't that a wonderful surprise?"

"Well, now, it sure is. A record, imagine! That's a real nice thing to find! What record is it?"

"Perry Como, singing *You Are My Sunshine*."

"Well, I'll be darned. I always liked that tune." Some raw carrots were lying on the table. Dad picked up a small one, scrubbed it on his chest, and took a bite. "How did Thelma happen to find it?"

"Oh, you know – just looking around for new things."

"M'm." Dad chewed the carrot. "Say, who has that picture we found a while back? I kind of liked it – that old clipper sailing along . . ."

"The Smiths. Next week the Sipichs get it, and they give the Smiths old McIntyre's music-box, and we give the Sipichs . . ." and she went down the tentative order of things that would exchange hands among the women at church this Sunday.

He nodded. "Looks like we can't have the picture for a while, I guess. Look, honey, you might try to get that detective book back from the Reillys. I was so busy the week we had it, I never got to finish all the stories . . ."

"I'll try," his wife said doubtfully. "But I hear the van Husens have a stereoscope they found in their cellar." Her voice was just a little accusing. "They had it two whole months before they told anybody about it . . "

"Say," Dad said, looking interested. "That'd be nice, too. Lots of pictures?"

"I suppose so. I'll see on Sunday. I'd like to have it – but we still owe the van Husens for their canary. I don't know why that bird had to pick *our* house to die . . . it must have been sick when we got it. Now there's just no satisfying Betty van Husen – she even hinted she'd like our *piano* for a while!"

"Well, honey, you try for the stereoscope – or just anything you think we'll like." At last he swallowed the carrot. It had been a little young and tough. Anthony's whims about the weather made it so that people never knew what crops would come up, or what shape they'd be in if they did. All they could do was plant a lot; and always enough of something came up any one season to live on. Just once there had been a grain surplus; tons of it had been hauled to the edge of Peaksville and dumped off into the nothingness. Otherwise, nobody could have breathed, when it started to spoil.

"You know," Dad went on. "It's nice to have the new things around. It's nice to think that there's probably still a lot of stuff nobody's found yet, in cellars and attics and barns and down behind things. They help, somehow. As much as anything can help . . ."

"Sh-h!" Mom glanced nervously around.

"Oh," Dad said, smiling hastily. "It's all right! The new things are *good*! It's *nice* to be able to have something around you've never seen before, and know that something you've given somebody else is making them happy . . .that's a real *good* thing."

"A good thing," his wife echoed.

"Pretty soon," Aunt Amy said, from the stove, "there won't be any more new things. We'll have found everything there is to find. Goodness, that'll be too bad . . ."

"*Amy!*"

"Well . . ." her pale eyes were shallow and fixed, a sign of her recurrent vagueness. "It will be kind of a shame – no new things . . ."

"Don't *talk* like that," Mom said, trembling. "Amy, be *quiet*!"

"It's *good*," said Dad, in the loud, familiar, wanting-to-be-over-heard tone of voice. "Such talk is *good*. It's okay, honey – don't you see? It's good for Amy to talk any way she wants. It's good for her to feel bad. Everything's good. Everything *has* to be good . . ."

Anthony's mother was pale. And so was Aunt Amy – the peril of the moment had suddenly penetrated the clouds surrounding her mind. Sometimes it was difficult to handle words so that they might not prove disastrous. You just never *knew*. There were so many things it was wise not to say, or even think – but remonstration for saying or thinking them might be just as bad, if Anthony heard and decided to do anything about it. You could just never tell what Anthony was liable to do.

Everything had to be good. Had to be fine just as it was, even if it wasn't. Always. Because any change might be worse. So terribly much worse.

"Oh, my goodness, yes, of course it's good," Mom said. "You talk any way you want to, Amy, and it's just fine. Of course, you want to remember that some ways are *better* than others . . ."

Aunt Amy stirred the peas, fright in her pale eyes.

"Oh, yes," she said. "But I don't feel like talking right now. It . . . it's *good* that I don't feel like talking."

Dad said tiredly, smiling, "I'm going out to wash up."

They started arriving around eight. By that time, Mom and Aunt Amy had the big table in the dining-room set, and two more tables off to the side. The candles were burning, and the chairs placed, and Dad had a big fire going in the fireplace.

The first to arrive were the Sipichs, John and Mary. John wore his best suit, and was well-scrubbed and pink-faced after his day in McIntyre's pasture. The suit was neatly pressed, but getting threadbare at elbows and cuffs. Old McIntyre was working on a loom, designing from school-books, but so far it was slow going. McIntyre was a capable man with wood and tools, but a loom was a big order when you couldn't get metal parts.

McIntyre had been one of the ones who, at first, had wanted to try to get Anthony to make things the villagers needed, like clothes and canned goods and medical supplies and gasoline. Since then, he felt that what had happened to the whole Terrance family and Joe Kinney was his fault, and he worked hard trying to make it up to the rest of them. And since then, no one had tried to get Anthony to do anything.

Mary Sipich was a small, cheerful woman in a simple dress. She immediately set about helping Mom and Aunt Amy put the finishing touches on the dinner.

The next arrivals were the Smiths and the Dunns, who lived right next to each other down the road, only a few yards from the nothingness. They drove up in the Smiths' wagon, drawn by their old horse.

Then the Reillys showed up, from across the darkened wheatfield, and the evening really began. Pat Reilly sat down at the big upright in the front room, and began to play from the popular sheet music on the rack. He played softly, as expressively as he could – and nobody sang.

Anthony liked piano playing a whole lot, but not singing; often he would come up from the basement, or down from the attic, or just *come*, and sit on top of the piano, nodding his head as Pat played *Lover* or *Boulevard of Broken Dreams* or *Night and Day*. He seemed to prefer ballads, sweet-sounding songs – but the one time somebody had started to sing, Anthony had looked over from the top of the piano and done something that made everybody afraid of singing from then on. Later, they'd decided that the piano was what Anthony had heard first, before anybody had ever tried to sing, and now anything else added to it didn't sound right and distracted him from his pleasure.

So, every television night, Pat would play the piano, and that was the beginning of the evening. Wherever Anthony was, the music would make him happy, and put him in a good mood, and he would know that they were gathering for television and waiting for him.

By 8.30 everybody had shown up, except for the 17 children and Mrs. Soames who was off watching them in the school-house at the far end of town. The children of Peaksville were never, never allowed near the Fremont house – not since little Fred Smith had tried to play with Anthony on a dare. The younger children weren't even told about Anthony. The others had mostly forgotten about him, or were told that he was a nice, nice goblin but they must never go near him.

Dan and Ethel Hollis came late, and Dan walked in not suspecting a thing. Pat Reilly had played the piano until his hands ached – he'd worked pretty hard with them today – and now he got up and everybody gathered around to wish Dan Hollis a happy birthday.

"Well I'll be darned," Dan grinned. "This is swell. I wasn't expecting this at all . . . gosh, this is *swell*!"

They gave him his presents – mostly things they had made by hand, though some were things that people had possessed as their own and now gave him as his. John Sipich gave him a watch charm, hand-carved out of a piece of hickory wood. Dan's watch had broken down a year or so ago, and there was nobody in the village who knew how to fix it, but he still carried it around because it had been his grandfather's and was a fine old heavy thing of gold and silver. He attached the charm to the chain, while everybody laughed and said John had done a nice job of carving. Then Mary Sipich gave him a knitted necktie, which he put on, removing the one he'd worn.

The Reillys gave him a little box they had made, to keep things in. They didn't say what things, but Dan said he'd keep his personal jewellery in it. The Reillys had made it out of a cigar box, having carefully peeled off its paper and lined it on the inside with velvet. The outside had been polished, and carefully if not expertly carved by Pat – but his carving got complimented too. Dan Hollis received many other gifts – a pipe, a pair of shoelaces, a tie pin, a knitted pair of socks, some fudge, a pair of garters made from old suspenders.

He unwrapped each gift with vast pleasure, and wore as many of them as he could right there, even the garters. He lit up the pipe, and said he'd never had a better smoke; which wasn't quite true, because the pipe wasn't broken in yet. Peter Manners had had it lying around ever since he'd received it as a gift four years ago from an out-of-town relative who hadn't known he'd stopped smoking.

Dan put the tobacco into the bowl very carefully. Tobacco was precious. It was only pure luck that Pat Reilly had decided to try to grow some in his backyard just before what had happened to Peaksville had happened. It didn't grow very well, and then they had to cure it and shred it and all, and it was just precious stuff. Everybody in town used wooden holders old McIntyre had made, to save on butts.

Last of all, Thelma Dunn gave Dan Hollis the record she had found.

Dan's eyes misted even before he opened the package. He knew it was a record.

"Gosh," he said softly. "What one is it? I'm almost afraid to look . . ."

"You haven't got it, darling," Ethel Hollis smiled. "Don't you remember, I asked about *You Are My Sunshine*?"

"Oh, gosh," Dan said again. Carefully he removed the wrapping and stood there fondling the record, running his big hands over the worn grooves with their tiny, dulling crosswise scratches. He looked around the room, eyes shining, and they all smiled back, knowing how delighted he was.

"Happy birthday, darling!" Ethel said, throwing her arms around him and kissing him.

He clutched the record in both hands, holding it off to one side as she pressed against him. "Hey," he laughed, pulling back his head. "Be careful . . . I'm holding a priceless object!" He looked around again, over his wife's arms, which were still around his neck. His eyes were hungry. "Look . . . do you think we could play it? Lord, what I'd give to hear some new music . . . just the first part, the orchestral part, before Como sings?"

Faces sobered. After a minute, John Sipich said, "I don't think we'd better, Dan. After all, we don't know just where the singer comes in – it'd be taking too much of a chance. Better wait till you get home."

Dan Hollis reluctantly put the record on the buffet with all his other presents. "It's *good*," he said automatically, but disappointedly, "that I can't play it here."

"Oh, yes," said Sipich. "It's good." To compensate for Dan's disappointed tone, he repeated, "It's *good*."

* * *

They ate dinner, the candles lighting their smiling faces, and ate it all right down to the last delicious drop of gravy. They complimented Mom and Aunt Amy on the roast beef, and the peas and carrots, and the tender corn on the cob. The corn hadn't come from the Fremont's cornfield, naturally – everybody knew what was out there; and the field was going to weeds.

Then they polished off the desert – homemade ice cream and cakes. And then they sat back, in the flickering light of the candles, and chatted, waiting for television.

There was never a lot of mumbling on television night – everybody came and had a good dinner at the Fremont's, and that was nice, and afterwards there was television, and nobody really thought much about that – it just had to be put up with. So it was a pleasant enough get-together, aside from your having to watch what you said just as carefully as you always did everywhere. If a dangerous thought came into your mind, you just started mumbling, even right in the middle of a sentence. When you did that, the others just ignored you until you felt happier again and stopped.

Anthony liked television night. He had only done two or three awful things on television night in the whole past year.

Mom had put a bottle of brandy on the table, and they each had a tiny glass of it. Liquor was even more precious than tobacco. The villagers could make wine, but the grapes weren't right, and certainly the techniques weren't, and it wasn't very good wine. There were only a few bottles of real liquor left in the village – four rye, three Scotch, three brandy, nine real wine and half a bottle of Drambuie belonging to old McIntyre (only for marriages) – and when those were gone, that was it.

Afterward, everybody wished that the brandy hadn't been brought out. Because Dan Hollis drank more of it than he should have, and mixed it with a lot of the homemade wine. Nobody thought anything about it at first, because he didn't show it much outside, and it was his birthday party and a happy party, and Anthony liked these get-togethers and shouldn't see any reason to do anything even if he was listening.

But Dan Hollis got high, and did a silly thing. If they'd seen it coming, they'd have taken him outside and walked him around.

The first thing they knew, Dan stopped laughing right in the middle of the story about how Thelma Dunn had found the Perry Como record and dropped it and it hadn't broken because she'd moved faster than she ever had before in her life and caught it. He was fondling the record again, and looking longingly at the Fremonts' gramophone over in the corner, and suddenly he stopped laughing and his face got slack, and then it got ugly, and he said, "Oh, *Christ*!"

Immediately the room was still. So still they could hear the whirring movement of the grandfather clock out in the hall. Pat Reilly had been playing the piano, softly. He stopped, his hands poised over the yellowed keys.

The candles on the dining-room table flickered in a cool breeze that blew through the lace curtains over the bay window.

"Keep playing, Pat," Anthony's father said softly.

Pat started again. He played *Night and Day*, but his eyes were sidewise on Dan Hollis, and he missed notes.

Dan stood in the middle of the room, holding the record. In his other hand he held a glass of brandy so hard his hand shook.

They were all looking at him.

"*Christ*," he said again, and he made it sound like a dirty word.

Reverend Younger, who had been talking with Mom and Aunt Amy by the dining-room door, said "Christ" too – but he was using it in a prayer. His hands were clasped, and his eyes were closed.

John Sipich moved forward. "Now, Dan . . . it's *good* for you to talk that way. But you don't want to talk too much, you know."

Dan shook off the hand Sipich put on his arm.

"Can't even play my record," he said loudly. He looked down at the record, and then around at their faces. "Oh, my *God* . . ."

He threw the glassful of brandy against the wall. It splattered and ran down the wallpaper in streaks.

Some of the women gasped.

"Dan," Sipich said in a whisper. "Dan, cut it out . . ."

Pat Reilly was playing *Night and Day* louder, to cover up the sounds of the talk. It wouldn't do any good, though, if Anthony was listening.

Dan Hollis went over to the piano and stood by Pat's shoulder, swaying a little.

"Pat," he said. "Don't play *that*. Play *this*." And he began to sing. Softly, hoarsely, miserably: "Happy birthday to me . . . Happy birthday to me . . ."

"Dan!" Ethel Hollis screamed. She tried to run across the room to him. Mary Sipich grabbed her arm and held her back. "Dan," Ethel screamed again. "Stop . . ."

"My God, be quiet!" hissed Mary Sipich, and pushed her towards one of the men, who put his hand over her mouth and held her still.

". . . Happy birthday, dear Danny," Dan sang. "Happy birthday . . . to me!" He stopped and looked down at Pat Reilly. "Play it, Pat. Play it, so I can sing right . . . you know I can't carry a tune unless somebody plays it!"

Pat Reilly put his hands on the keys and began *Lover* – in a slow waltz tempo, the way Anthony liked it. Pat's face was white. His hands fumbled.

Dan Hollis stared over at the dining-room door. At Anthony's mother, and at Anthony's father who had gone to join her.

"*You* had him," he said. Tears gleamed on his cheeks as the candle-light caught them. "*You* had to go and *have* him . . ."

He closed his eyes, and the tears squeezed out. He sang loudly, "You are my sunshine . . . my only sunshine . . . you make me happy . . . when I am blue . . . "

Anthony *came* into the room.

Pat stopped playing. He froze. Everybody froze. The breeze rippled the curtains. Ethel Hollis couldn't even try to scream – she had fainted.

"Please don't take my sunshine . . . away . . ." Dan's voice faltered into silence. His eyes widened. He put both hands out in front of him, the empty glass in one, the record in the other. He hiccupped, and said, "*No* . . ."

"Bad man," Anthony said, and thought Dan Hollis into something like nothing anyone would have believed possible, and then he thought the thing into a grave deep, deep in the cornfield.

The glass and record thumped on the rug. Neither broke.

Anthony's purple gaze went around the room.

Some of the people began mumbling. They all tried to smile. The sound of mumbling filled the room like a far-off approval. Out of the murmuring came one or two clear voices:

"Oh, it's a very *good* thing," said John Sipich.

"A good thing," said Anthony's father, smiling. He'd had more practice in smiling than most of them. "A wonderful thing."

"It's swell . . . just swell," said Pat Reilly, tears leaking from eyes and nose, and he began to play the piano again, softly, his trembling hands feeling for *Night and Day*.

Anthony climbed up on top of the piano, and Pat played for two hours.

* * *

Afterwards, they watched television. They all went into the front room, and lit just a few candles, and pulled up chairs around the set. It was a small-screen set, and they couldn't all sit close enough to it to see, but that didn't matter. They didn't even turn the set on. It wouldn't have worked anyway, there being no electricity in Peaksville.

They just sat silently, and watched the twisting, writhing shapes on the screen, and listened to the sounds that came out of the speaker, and none of them had any idea of what it was all about. They never did. It was always the same.

"It's real nice," Aunt Amy said once, her pale eyes on the meaningless flickers and shadows. "But I liked it a little better when there were cities outside and we could get real . . ."

"Why, Amy!" said Mom. "It's good for you to say such a thing. Very good. But how can you mean it? Why, this television is *much* better than anything we ever used to get!"

"Yes," chimed in John Sipich. "It's fine. It's the best show we've ever seen!"

He sat on the couch, with two other men, holding Ethel Hollis flat against the cushions, holding her arms and legs and putting their hands over her mouth, so she couldn't start screaming again.

"It's really *good*!" he said again.

Mom looked out of the front window, across the darkened road, across Henderson's darkened wheatfield to the vast, endless, grey nothingness in which the little village of Peaksville floated like a soul – the huge nothingness that was most evident at night, when Anthony's brassy day had gone.

It did no good to wonder where they were . . . no good at all. Peaksville was just somewhere. Somewhere away from the world. It was wherever it had been since that day three years ago when Anthony had crept from her womb and old Doc Bates – God rest him – had screamed and dropped him and tried to kill him, and Anthony had whined and done the thing. Had taken the village somewhere. Or had destroyed the world and left only the village, nobody knew which.

It did no good to wonder about it. Nothing at all did any good – except to live as they must live. Must always, always live, if Anthony would let them. These thoughts were dangerous, she thought.

She began to mumble. The others started mumbling too. They had all been thinking, evidently.

The men on the couch whispered and whispered to Ethel Hollis, and when they took their hands away, she mumbled too.

While Anthony sat on top of the set and made television, they sat around and mumbled and watched the meaningless, flickering shapes far into the night.

Next day it snowed, and killed off half the crops – but it was a *good* day.

FREDRIC BROWN HAS THE LAST WORD . . .

The end

PROFESSOR JONES had been working on time theory for many years.

"And I have found the key equation," he told his daughter one day. "Time is a field. This machine I have made can manipulate, even reverse, that field."

Pushing a button as he spoke, he said, "This should make time run backward run time make should this," said he, spoke he as button a pushing.

"Field that, reverse even, manipulate can made have I machine this. Field a is time." Day one daughter his told he, "Equation key the found have I and."

Years many for theory time on working been had Jones Professor.

END THE